# Bible Positions
# on
# Political Issues

# by
# JOHN HAGEE

Books by Pastor John Hagee

# Bible Positions
# on
# Political Issues

### by
## JOHN HAGEE

First printing, November 1992

# Contents

# Chapter 1

# Abortion: The American Holocaust

Abortion is a very emotional and controversial subject. Our purpose in this message is to discover God's view of abortion as reflected in the scripture.

I am not interested in the opinion of the ACLU about abortion. I am not interested in the opinion of the feminist movement about abortion. I do not want to know the Supreme Court's position on abortion. I do not want to know the Republican Party or the Democratic Party platform on abortion. I want to know God's position on abortion, because his is the only opinion that matters.

The questions we will answer from God's word are these: Is the fetus considered human life? When is life recognizable in the womb? Is there a penalty to pay for loss of life in the womb? Does the fetus have personality, or is it a blob of flesh? Does the woman have the right of her own body over the fetus? Is there a judgment on legislators who pass legislation making godless things possible? Is the nation that lives contrary to the word of God brought directly under a curse and under the wrath of God? Does God expect believers to help those who are defenseless?

There is a lack of knowledge in the body of Christ about abortion. There is no lack of emotion or opinion, but there is a lack of knowledge. Let me tell you something up front. If the Supreme Court ruled tomorrow that abortion was illegal, we would still need to convince the American people in their thinking and their attitude that abortion is wrong before God. The law will not bring instant purity. Purity only comes when the heart of the nation is determined to live according to the dictates of God.

I appreciate the efforts that are made to get the Supreme Court to stand firmly against abortion. But understand that it is not a panacea. If the Supreme Court said "no more abortions," there would still be hundreds of thousands of abortions because people in their hearts and their thinking are in rebellion against the law of God.

## Destroyed for a lack of knowledge

Hosea 4:6 says, "My people are destroyed for lack of knowledge: because thou hast rejected knowledge, I will also reject thee, that thou shalt be no priest to me: seeing thou hast forgotten the law of thy God, I will also forget thy children."

The word translated *destroyed* in this verse is the Hebrew word *dâmâh*. It means to be silent, and hence to perish, to fail or be defeated. So another translation of Hosea 4:6 would be, "My people will be silent, and hence they will fail or perish, or be defeated for a lack of knowledge."

Again, there is a lack of knowledge within the body of Christ on the subject of abortion—not a lack of opinion or emotion, but a lack of knowledge. The Bible does not say, as some people think, that truth will make you free. It says that the *knowledge* of the truth will make you free. "You shall know the truth, and the truth shall make you free" (John 8:32).

Truth is not what I say it is. Truth is not what you think it is. Truth is what God's word says, and it's not truth until God's word does say it. Paul said it quite plainly: "Let God be true, but every man a liar" (Romans 3:4).

We need to see abortion as God sees it. His opinion is plainly recorded in scripture. And once we know it, we are honor bound to not remain silent, but to do all we can to bring God's opinion about abortion to the forefront in our society. If we remain silent, then we will be defeated for a lack of knowledge, as Hosea said.

The great handicap of the American church is that we have learned to be silent in the day of adversity. You have heard it said, "All that is required for the triumph of evil is for good men to say nothing." My position is that God's word is the truth. And the moment you reject truth you have embraced a lie.

So our purpose is to gather truth from the word of God. We will formulate God's opinion by examining his testimony, much as we would search for the preponderance of evidence in a court-room trial.

## God's opinion of children

Look first at the fourth chapter of Jonah, which demonstrates God's unlimited love.

Jonah has been commissioned of the Lord to go to Nineveh with a message of repentance. Now Nineveh was the enemy of Israel, much like Russia has been the enemy of America in the past. Jonah had absolutely no love for Nineveh. What he had was a one-word message from God: repent.

So Jonah went and preached his message "repent," after God gave him a one-way ride in Shamu to get him where he needed to go. And to Jonah's shock and amazement, Nineveh repented.

The king commanded everyone in that pagan country to fast and repent. He told them to put on sackcloth and ashes and to eat no bread and drink no water and to repent before God. So God sent forgiveness and revival to the land.

Was Jonah happy that Nineveh heeded his message and repented? Not at all. Jonah was so angry he pouted. He went out and sat under a juniper tree and began to pout because God didn't do what Jonah had wanted him to do.

The Lord answered Jonah's complaint in verse 11:

*And should not I spare Nineveh, that great city, wherein are more than sixscore thousand persons that cannot discern between their right hand and their left hand?*

God said he had spared Nineveh because there were 120,000 people who couldn't tell their right hands from their left hands. Now who would that describe? Children.

What God was saying to Jonah is this, "I'm sparing Nineveh for the 120,000 children there." This shows us God's opinion about children.

What did Jesus say about children?

*Suffer the little children, and forbid them not, to come unto me: for of such is the kingdom of heaven.*
Matthew 19:14

The word of God gives a very loving, compassionate position to children. God the Father and his Son love children. In his teaching, Jesus blessed the children. He picked them up, he kissed them and embraced them. Should we not have the same love and compassion for children?

God's word always makes special provision for the preservation of children. The Old Testament manner of providing for children and their mothers was gleaning the fields.

A farmer was not permitted to go over his fruit trees more than once during the harvest. Then the widows and orphans were allowed to beat the trees and gather whatever they could shake down. It was a way of preserving them by providing for them out of the abundance of God's blessing.

The Bible says that angels defend children, and that children are the heritage of the Lord. For those who believe the Judeo-Christian ethic, children have a very exalted, holy position. Children are precious to the Lord.

### Is a fetus a life?

Abortion is the termination of a pregnancy and the destruction of a fetus, a developing human being. Before *Roe v. Wade*, abortions were illegal in most states and were customarily performed only for extreme reasons. But on January 22, 1973, a day of infamy in American history, the Supreme Court of the United States reversed the legal position on abortion. Abortions were allowed any time during the first six months of a pregnancy, and in some cases after that.

Every year since then, there have been approximately 1.5 million abortions per year in America. In twenty years, at the rate of over 4,000 babies each day, we will have slaughtered 30 million unborn American citizens. Picture in your mind a city *30 times* the population of San Antonio, Texas, my "home town" and the ninth largest city in America. That's how many unborn American children have been killed.

The abortionists say, "Well, they're not really children. The fetus is just a blob of tissue." What does God's word have to say about that? Leviticus 17:11, "For the life of the flesh is in the blood," and verse 14, "For it is the life of all flesh; the blood of it is for the life thereof." God is saying in these two verses that where there is blood, there is life.

God is the giver of life. He says that where there is blood, there is life. Medical science has the ability to detect life in the womb on the twelfth day after conception. That's only because medical science is a long way behind God. God, who is its architect, can instantly detect life. Please understand that you don't start living on the twelfth day, just because that's when medical science can detect life. You start living instantly, according to the word of God, from the moment of conception.

The finest scientific minds in the world can call a fetus a blob of tissue. It makes no difference. God still calls it life.

Some of you reading this may have had an abortion in the past. I am not trying to put a guilt trip on you or place you under condemnation. God can and will forgive you for your participation, willing or unwilling, in an abortion. If you haven't asked him before now, I pray you will. God loves you and wants to restore you, and wants to reunite you with that aborted child in eternity.

## God says, "don't sacrifice your children"

God's word very specifically says that there are some things he hates. Leviticus 18 has a list of things God hates; one of them is child sacrifice. Verse 21 says Israel was not to sacrifice their children to Molech, the pagan god. "And thou shalt not let any of thy seed," your children, "pass through the fire to Molech."

Not many children in America are sacrificed as burnt offerings, although that's exactly what some satanists do. But 1.5 million children each year are burned alive in abortion clinics with saline solutions, or crushed with forceps, or violently torn apart by suction machines.

I want to quote here a passage from a recent book by Carol Everett, a former abortion clinic operator. (The book is called **Scarlet Lady, Confessions of A Successful Abortionist**, and is published by Wolgemuth & Hyatt. I highly recommend the book. Ask for it at your Christian bookstore.)

Carol Everett, now a full-time pro-lifer, says she ran "the Neiman Marcus of abortion clinics." She was quite successful until forced out of the business after several botched abortions, at least one of them fatal, at her clinics. The medical records were altered so the clinic wouldn't be sued.

Here's how she describes one of the botched procedures.

> *I went to check out the operating room to be sure it was ready. The instruments had to be prepared—large dilators, sterilized yet cool enough; a #16 cannula, a tube to insert into the uterus; and Bierhoff forceps, to remove the pieces of the unwanted baby.* (page 22)

You see, this "blob of tissue" has recognizable little arms and legs. The nurse or operating assistant has to lay out the "pieces" after the abortion to make sure none of the "blob of tissue" was left inside the woman to cause complications.

Continuing with the story…

> *After the anesthetist put her to sleep, I placed my hand on Jenni's abdomen. I felt movement, one of the only babies I can ever remember feeling move inside the*

*mother during an abortion.*

*Harvey proceeded as normal: He cleaned off the cervix with Betadine, dilated the cervix, and suctioned briefly to break the bag of amniotic fluid surrounding the baby. The baby did not move again after he finished suctioning. The next step required Harvey to crush the baby inside Jenni's uterus and then remove the baby piece by piece using Bierhoff forceps.*

*The first time Harvey reached in, he pulled out placenta. The second time he reached in, he pulled out the lining around the colon. Immediately, I saw the shock on Harvey's face."* (page 23)

An innocent, "safe and legal" medical procedure to remove a "blob of tissue?" This botched abortion resulted in a colostomy for the twenty-one year old patient.

## Inside the abortion mills

Another abortion was recalled this way.

*Painful as it was to admit, I knew we were not helping women have safe abortions; instead, we were maiming and even killing them. How had this happened?*

*I remember another patient, a twenty-seven year old from a small town in Arkansas who came in with her parents. She thought she was about twenty weeks pregnant at the time. Dr. Johnson, who examined her, determined he could do the abortion.*

*Using local anesthesia and a small dosage of Valium, Harvey started the abortion, but he discovered the baby was too far advanced. Its muscle structure was so strong that the baby would not come apart. After almost an hour on the table with six nurses holding and pulling the woman away from Harvey, the baby's body finally separated from the head and came out. Then Harvey worked and worked to crush the head and remove it. It was a very long ordeal for both the woman and Dr. Johnson.*

*One of the nurses, Becky, who never reacted to anything, rolled her eyes back in her head; I thought for a minute she was going to faint.*

*After the procedure, Harvey measured the baby's foot. He tried to hide the measurement from me, but I saw it—the baby was about thirty-two weeks, probably old enough to survive outside its mother.*

*The baby's body was too large to go down the garbage disposal, so Harvey suggested I take it to our competitor's trash receptacle so that if it were found, it would be in his trash—not ours. Dutifully, I wrapped the baby in a paper drape, put it in a brown paper sack, and planted it in the other clinic's trash that night.* (pages 29-30)

That's an inside look at American abortion mills. Anyone who takes the time to read Carol Everett's book will clearly understand that abortion is not about women's rights. It's about money, lots of money. It is nothing less than murder for hire, sanctified by the Supreme Court of the United States.

## Satan always attacks the children

Jesus said, "I am come that [you] might have life" (John 10:10). What does Satan come to do? The same verse says the thief [Satan] comes to steal, kill and to destroy.

Think of the attacks on children in the history of civilization. Remember Pharoah who attacked the Hebrew children and drowned the male babies in the Nile river. Remember Herod who slaughtered the children under two years old, trying to stop Jesus Christ from living to die for the sins of the world.

It is Satan who has the attack of America's children in his mind. The children of our nation are under the most insidious attack in the history of America. If they escape the abortion mill, there's the drug pusher on the corner. There's the Satanist trying to recruit them in high school.

Our children are up against it from every front. God's word says, "Suffer the little children. Love them. Nurture them." Satan's objective is to kill them. Which viewpoint seems to be having its way in America today?

## The land is defiled

Look again at the passage of scripture in Leviticus 18:

*And thou shalt not let any of thy seed pass through the fire to Molech...Thou shalt not lie with mankind, as with womankind: it is abomination. Neither shalt thou lie with any beast to defile thyself therewith... Defile not ye yourselves in any of these things: for in all these the nations are defiled which I cast out before you: And the land is defiled: therefore I do visit the iniquity thereof upon it, and the land itself vomiteth out her inhabitants. Ye shall therefore keep my statutes and my judgments, and shall not commit any of these abominations; neither any of your own nation, nor any stranger that sojourneth among you: (For all these abominations have the men of the land done, which were before you, and the land is defiled;) That the land spew not you out also, when ye defile it, as it spewed out the nations that were before you.* (verses 21-28)

God says when these things happen in your nation, the land is defiled. Do you know anything about the justice and holiness of God? Let me tell you, whenever God gets fed up with a nation, here are the things that happen in rather rapid succession.

One, he begins by sending drought. This is the pattern in the Old Testament. After he sends drought, he sends floods. After he sends floods, he sends earthquakes. After earthquakes, then economic depression.

We have had droughts in the United States. Last year we had floods in the United States. This year we're having hurricanes and more earthquakes. California can't stop shaking. And the next thing that is coming is economic destruction of these United States.

Why? Because of the blood of the children murdered in America's abortion clinics. God is saying to this country, "I hear the blood of the innocent crying. I see the tear of every child murdered in its mother's womb. I am their avenger and your land is under judgment because you have taken the life I have given and destroyed it. Now you must answer for it."

The wrath of God is not coming to America. The wrath of God is already on this nation and it is only going to get worse.

## Abortion: the American Holocaust

I want to compare Adolf Hitler and the Holocaust to what is happening with abortion in America. Abortion is the American Holocaust. The comparison is plain. Six million Jews exterminated in Hitler's Germany. Almost thirty million in America's abortion clinics (we've simply been at it longer).

Hitler taught that Jews were sub-human. I won't go into the details of Nazi philosophy, but that's what they believed: Jews were not human beings. On the American side of the ledger, unborn babies are not human, they're a "blob of tissue."

Hitler killed the Jews in mass. America is slaughtering babies at the rate of over 4,000 every day. Hitler used the ashes of the Jews to make bars of soap. American abortion clinics sell fetal tissue to use in the manufacture of cosmetics, as well as for medical research. What's the difference?

Don't turn up your nose at Hitler. We're no better, we're worse. Don't look at Joseph Mengele's medical experiments on Jewish children and say you're shocked. Every doctor and every nurse who performs abortions is the modern medical equivalent of Joseph Mengele.

## The price for harming life in the womb

We have already seen that the fetus is alive and not just a "blob of tissue." God says that not only is the fetus alive, but there is a price to pay for harming the unborn child in the womb.

*If men strive, and hurt a woman with child, so that her fruit depart from her* [so that she has a miscarriage or an aborted pregnancy], *and yet no mischief follow: he shall be surely punished, according as the woman's husband will lay upon him; and he shall pay as the judges determine. And if any mischief follow* [if any harm or injury occurs], *then thou shalt give life for life.* Exodus 21:22-23

God says here that if you hurt a pregnant woman and she loses the baby, you have to pay a penalty—not because it was a "blob of tissue," but because it was life.

Let's look at Isaiah to see what else God says about the value of life in the womb.

*The Lord hath called me from the womb...And now, saith the Lord that formed me from the womb to be his servant...* Isaiah 49:1, 5

God did not speak to a lifeless blob, but to a living child in the womb. God called Jeremiah, as well as Isaiah, to be a prophet while he was still in his mother's womb.

*Then the word of the Lord came unto me, saying, Before I formed thee in the belly I knew thee; and before thou camest forth out of the womb I sanctified thee, and I ordained thee a prophet unto the nations.* Jeremiah 1:4-5

Would God name and ordain a meaningless blob? That unborn child in the womb is not a blob of flesh, but a life sophisticated enough for God Almighty to have a relationship with it.

Read the story of the birth of John the Baptist in the first chapter of Luke. Verse 15 says, "For he shall be great in the sight of the Lord, and shall drink neither wine nor strong drink [just like all Baptists]; and he shall be filled with the Holy Ghost [just like all Pentecostals], even from his mother's womb."

John the Baptist had a charismatic experience while he was still in his mother's womb. Verse 41 says he "*leaped* in her womb!" This unborn child—not a meaningless blob, but a child—leaped at the presence of the Holy Spirit as he responded to the power of God in his mother's life.

### God knows the future of life in the womb

In the 25th chapter of Genesis, God looks at the fetal life in the womb of Rebekah and tells the future of her two children, Esau and Jacob.

> *And Isaac entreated the Lord for his wife, because she was barren: and the Lord was entreated of him, and Rebekah his wife conceived. And the children struggled together within her; and she said, If it be so, why am I thus? And she went to enquire of the Lord.* Genesis 25:21-22

This was a divine sonogram. The Lord looked in her womb and told her what was going on.

> *And the Lord said unto her, Two nations are in thy womb, and two manner of people shall be separated from thy bowels; and the one people shall be stronger than the other people; and the elder shall serve the younger.* Genesis 25:23

When God looked into Rebekah's womb, he did not see a meaningless blob of flesh. He saw two children. He knew their names. He knew their destiny. He knew their character. He knew their temperament.

He knew them because they were alive. He knew them because they were people. He knew them because they had souls, and he had a divine purpose for them. They were not tissue to be put down the garbage disposal of some abortion clinic. They were vessels of God, holy and precious, and they deserved the right to live.

## Children are God's reward

Here's a passage to memorize and quote when your children pull the drapes off the wall and break the treasures you've been saving for twenty years.

> *Lo, children are a heritage of the Lord: and the fruit of the womb is his reward. As arrows are in the hand of a mighty man; so are children of the youth. Happy is the man that hath his quiver full of them.*    Psalm 127:3-5

Let me tell you some things that don't make sense to me. If children are the heritage of the Lord, and that's what the word of God says, then why do we protect animals and slaughter babies in this country?

Why is it that the crowd who is against the death penalty is for abortion? What kind of logic is it to want murderers to live and innocent babies to die? I don't get it. It's absolutely convoluted reasoning.

It makes no sense other than to know that it's demonic, it's ungodly, and it is time for every American to cease to be silent and to raise his voice. And it's time for every American to go to the voting booth and refuse to put any politician in any office who stands for abortion of any kind. Get them out of office now!

## Does the woman have the right over her body?

What about the argument that a woman has an absolute right over her own body? Again, let's look at what the scripture says.

> *Flee fornication. Every sin that a man doeth is without the body; but he that committeth fornication sinneth*

*against his own body. What? know ye not that your*
*body is the temple of the Holy Ghost which is in you,*
*which ye have of God, and ye are not your own? For*
*ye are bought with a price: therefore glorify God in*
*your body, and in your spirit, which are God's.*
1 Corinthians 6:18-19

"You are not your own...you are bought with a price." That's a very simple, clear Bible fact: your body does not belong to you. Once a baby is in your body, he is sharing your body, and that baby has a divine right to live according to the counsel of God.

## The right to life is older than the Constitution

What did Thomas Jefferson write in the Declaration of Independence about the right to life? "We hold these truths to be self-evident, that all men are created equal, that they are endowed by their Creator with certain unalienable rights, that among these are life, liberty, and the pursuit of happiness."

The right to life is a divine right, endowed by our Creator, the Declaration says. Before we ever had a Constitution, this country recognized the right to life. So when are we going to stop the slaughter of the innocent citizens of these United States and uphold the principles of our founding fathers? Our elected officials must be held accountable.

Proverbs 6:16-19 says there are six things the Lord hates. One, "a proud look." Two, "a lying tongue." Three, "hands that shed innocent blood." An unborn child is innocent. God hates the hands of the abortionist who sheds innocent blood.

God's judgment is upon legislators who pass legislation making godless things possible. This is clearly demonstrated in Isaiah 10:1, which says, "Woe to them that decree unrighteous decrees, and that write grievousness which they have prescribed."

God clearly says that legislators who pass unrighteous decrees have the judgment of God upon them. Now can you imagine why our government is in such chaos and confusion? It is because our legislators and judges are in such violation of the word of God.

Harry Truman, one of the last great presidents this nation has had, once said, "A group of donkeys couldn't have Washington in a greater mess than what it is now." God bless Harry Truman. Ollie North calls Washington "Sodom on the Potomac," and our legislators the "political potentates of pork and privilege." God bless Ollie North.

## Must believers help the defenseless?

Does God expect believers to help those who are defenseless? Let's read the testimony of God in the book of Proverbs.

> *Open thy mouth for the dumb in the cause of all such as are appointed to destruction. Open thy mouth, judge righteously, and plead the cause of the poor and needy.* Proverbs 31:8-9

God gives you a command to open your mouth. Remember the words of Hosea that we looked at earlier: "My people are destroyed because they are silent; hence they fail and perish for the lack of knowledge." God has told us to open our mouths and say something! If we want to obey God, we must come to the defense of the helpless.

And when we do, God has promised us a blessing.

> *Blessed is he that considereth the poor: the Lord will deliver him in time of trouble. The Lord will preserve him, and keep him alive; and he shall be blessed upon the earth: and thou wilt not deliver him unto the will of his enemies. The Lord will strengthen him upon the bed of languishing: thou wilt make all his bed in his sickness.* Psalm 41:1-3

There are three benefits here for those who help the oppressed and the exploited: deliverance, preservation and a blessed life.

In the gospels, Jesus reaffirmed that we are to help the oppressed and defenseless. In fact, he said that everlasting punishment is reserved for those who will not come to the aid of the defenseless.

> *Then shall he say also unto them on the left hand, Depart from me, ye cursed, into everlasting fire, prepared for the devil and his angels: For I was ahungered, and ye gave me no meat: I was thirsty, and ye gave me no drink: I was a stranger, and ye took me not in: naked, and ye clothed me not: sick, and in prison, and ye visited me not.*
>
> *Then shall they also answer him, saying, Lord, when saw we thee ahungered, or athirst, or a stranger, or naked, or sick, or in prison, and did not minister unto thee? Then shall he answer them, saying, Verily I say unto you, Inasmuch as ye did it not to one of the least of these, ye did it not to me. And these shall go away into everlasting punishment: but the righteous into life eternal.* Matthew 25:41-46

These are Jesus' words: "What you have done *to the least of these*, you have done to me." That should be a very sobering thought to every person involved in the abortion industry, and to our legislators.

## How can we stop the slaughter?

How can we stop this slaughter of the unborn?

First of all, stop voting for politicians who are pro-abortion. Then stop them from authorizing federal funds for abortion clinics.

Before you can do that, you have to participate in the political process by voting. Did you even vote in the last election? I am amazed at the number of professing evangelical Christians who will not even bother to vote.

When Christians learn to get involved, when they start going to the voting booth, then we'll see a change. If the 40 million evangelicals in America would vote pro-life and anti-abortion, then no President, Senator or Congressman could get to Washington without the evangelical vote. That's how it ought to be.

And as far as it is "politically correct" to be "pro-choice," let me tell you something. Hitler was pro-choice. He chose the Jews to go to Auschwitz. It wasn't their choice, it was his.

Murderers are pro-choice. They choose to stick a gun in your face and blow your head off. That's their choice.

The baby in your womb will not choose the saline solution that will burn away his skin. That's your choice. Pro-choice is an idiotic argument for someone who will not face the truth.

If we do not use our freedom to preserve our freedom, we will lose our freedom. We have enjoyed freedom for so long in America that we assume we are going to enjoy freedom forever. That's a false assumption.

Abortion is the shedding of innocent blood. And the shedding of innocent blood brings the curse of God on the land. We are living in a defiled land, under the judgment of God.

## God is the avenger of blood

God avenges innocent blood. When Cain slew Abel, God said, "The voice of thy brother's blood crieth unto me from the ground" (Genesis 4:10). This simply means that blood cries out to God for vengeance.

Innocent blood is something that God can hear, and God's curse will come for the shedding of innocent blood.

God refused to let King David, who was a man "after God's own heart," build the temple. Why? "Because thou art a bloody man," it says in 2 Samuel 16:8.

David was not called a bloody man because of the thousands of Philistines he had killed in combat under God's direction. He was called a bloody man because he had innocent blood on his hands. David had sent Uriah, the husband of Bathsheba, into the heat of battle with the premeditated idea that he would be killed. It was murder under the guise of a military operation.

Later David reminded Israel why God chastised them by

permitting them to be captured by a foreign power—they had shed innocent blood.

> *Yea, they sacrificed their sons and their daughters unto devils, and shed innocent blood, even the blood of their sons and of their daughters, whom they sacrificed unto the idols of Canaan: and the land was polluted with blood. Thus were they defiled with their own works, and went a whoring with their own inventions. Therefore was the wrath of the Lord kindled against his people, insomuch that he abhorred his own inheritance. And he gave them into the hand of the heathen; and they that hated them ruled over them.*
> Psalm 106:37-41

The wrath of the Lord was kindled against his people and he gave them into the hand of the heathen. Do you not see that the United States has been turned over to the hand of the heathen?

The United States of America is literally being drenched with drugs by foreign governments who know they can corrupt our children, destroy their minds and bodies, and make this a weak civilization. We have been inundated with drugs and think we've done something grand because Manuel Noriega is in jail. It's like trying to drain the ocean with a teacup!

Why is it that our legislators extend financial aid to foreign governments and give trade advantages that make it virtually impossible for American businessmen to compete? Are we not economically in the hands of foreign countries? Why has the Congress of the United States agreed that all third world debt will be repaid by the American citizens?

I suggest to you that when you defy the laws of God, God begins to turn the screws until it becomes so unbearable somebody finally gets the idea in their mind, "Hey, maybe we're not living right. Maybe God is displeased." In the name of God, we need to wake up before America as a nation is no more.

We have shed innocent blood and God will avenge it.

Why did Judas hang himself? The Bible clearly says it was because he had betrayed innocent blood.

*Then Judas, which had betrayed him, when he saw*
*that he was condemned, repented himself, and brought*
*again the thirty pieces of silver to the chief priests and*
*elders, Saying, I have sinned in that I have betrayed*
*the innocent blood.* Matthew 27:3-4

Judas threw down the thirty pieces of silver then went out and hanged himself. He had betrayed innocent blood.

ABC ran a special report recently on the emotional problems of people who work in abortion clinics. That report was confirmed in the book I quoted earlier, **The Scarlet Lady**. People who work in abortion clinics have emotional problems they cannot handle. Many of them gravitate to alcoholism.

When a baby is aborted, no bell tolls on earth. But don't feel secure that nothing has happened, because a loving God in heaven wrote that death down as murder in the first degree. He measures every drop of innocent blood and he will avenge it. He will avenge it with wrath.

That's why the wrath of God is on America. And God's wrath on America will become greater until there is repentance from the White House to the church house for the shedding of innocent blood in the nation's abortion mills.

## What about the malformed fetus?

What if the doctors say the fetus is malformed and will have a hideous birth defect? Is abortion okay then?

Let us look first at the medical evidence. This statement is from Dr. T. McKeown of the Royal Society of Medicine in Great Britain:

*The large majority of malformations are unpredictable,*
*and are likely to remain so because they result mainly*
*from accidents associated with fertilization, implan-*
*tation and early development...Few malformations*
*are recognized during pregnancy, and none at the*
*early stage when abortion is technically easy.*

Dale Evans Rogers wrote a book called **Angel Unaware** about their seriously deformed baby who lived only two years. Here is what she said about the experience:

> *Our baby came into the world with an appalling handicap...I believe with all my heart that God sent her on a two-year mission to our household, to strengthen us spiritually and to draw us closer together in the knowledge and love and fellowship of God.*
>
> *It has been said that tragedy and sorrow never leave us where they find us. In this instance, Roy and I are grateful to God for the privilege of learning some great lessons through his tiny messenger, Robin Elisabeth Rogers.*

A seriously handicapped child was considered by Roy and Dale Evans Rogers as a wonderful blessing from God. You see, they had the same view of life as God did—life, all life, is precious and holy.

When Diana was expecting our youngest son, Matthew, she called my office one day crying. She had been told by someone who worked in the church nursery that she had been exposed to German measles. She had told that to her obstetrician, who had flippantly said, "Let's get an abortion."

She called me crying and asking what to do. I said, "Put that doctor on the phone." I fired the doctor on the spot. Two weeks later we found out that the little girl who was supposed to have German measles only had a rash. Had we listened to that doctor, our son would have been in a trash can somewhere.

I tell you there is a greater medical authority than the guy downtown with a saline solution looking for a way to murder children. God says, "Give life a chance." He is the architect of life, and in God's providence, life is holy.

This is what the word of God says about life and about abortion. The word abortion may not have been used in the Bible, but as we have seen, the Bible has plenty to say about abortion.

We have also seen that when we as a nation violate the word of God, we bring his judgment on this nation. America's problem now is not the economy. America's problem is God.

God will not put up with sin. America has bathed its land in the blood of innocent children. Our land is defiled. That's not my opinion—it's God's opinion. The only thing that can stop the wrath of God is national repentance.

If there is not national repentance, there will be a national collapse orchestrated by the hand of God. It doesn't matter what Dan Rather or Sam Donaldson thinks, it doesn't matter if CNN is there with live coverage. The only thing that matters is what the word of God says. And the word of God says judgment will come to those who shed innocent blood.

# The War Against The Unborn

Every 21 seconds another child becomes a victim of the war against the unborn. The statistics are staggering: over 4,000 slain every day, 1.5 million every year. This war has claimed the lives of more Americans than all previous wars combined.

There are no graves we can visit, no public memorials, only dumpsters and incinerators where the mangled bodies of war casualties are quietly discarded in back alleys.

## A Declaration of War

On January 22, 1973 the United States Supreme Court handed down its decision in the landmark *Roe v. Wade* case. In a sweeping exercise of raw judicial power, the Court struck down the abortion laws of all fifty states, uprooting the very foundations of Western civilization and abrogating the Judeo-Christian belief that all human life possesses equal and intrinsic worth. In a decision that has drawn the criticism of constitutional authorities, the court held that a woman's fundamental "right to privacy" renders her the sole arbiter over the life of her unborn child.

In the years since the *Roe v. Wade* decision, over 25 million unborn children have been sacrificed on the altar of convenience. One out of every four pregnancies now ends in abortion, and 98% of them are for non-medical, elective reasons—i.e., they are "convenience" abortions, performed to protect the "mental health" of the mother who does not want the child within her womb.

The Supreme Court's abortion decision sanctioned a new "quality of life" ethic espoused by certain groups who advocate death as a solution to social problems. From abortion we are moving quickly to infanticide and euthanasia, conveniently ridding ourselves of those members of society who are unwanted, imperfect or unproductive. No longer recognizing the intrinsic value of life which comes from being created in the image and likeness of God, man has imposed his own standard by which the relative worth of life is measured.

The American public did not vote on this abortion on demand policy and no state had an abortion law as unrestricted as the Court's 1973 dictum. While the Court's ruling has been applied as law, it has by no means settled the debate which continues to rage over the abortion issue.

## The Second American Civil War

On March 6, 1857 the Supreme Court held that Dred Scott, a black slave, was the property of his owner and had no rights under the Constitution of the United States. The Court said the black man was not a "citizen" and therefore not protected by law.

Like the black man in the 19th century, the unborn child finds himself outside the protection of the Constitution. In *Roe v. Wade* the Court went out of its way to find that the unborn child was not a "person" in the legal sense.

The infamous Dred Scott decision was eventually overturned, but only after a long and bitter struggle in the courts and on the battlefield. The important victory was won in the hearts and minds of the American people. "I am personally opposed to slavery, but cannot impose my view on others," was exposed as a bankrupt argument which carried no weight against the moral evil of human bondage.

Americans rejected the "pro-choice" argument in the last century, and they are rejecting it again. Abortion, like slavery, cannot stand when measured against the principles of freedom and equality Americans hold most dear.

## Fetal development

*Weeks 1 & 2.* At the moment of conception, when the father's sperm and the mother's ovum unite, a genetically unique one-celled individual is created. This one cell contains all the genetic coding—some 46 chromosomes and 30,000 genes—which determines the new individual's sex, his hair and eye color, his skin, facial features, and even certain qualities of his personality and intelligence.

Growth begins within six to twelve hours after conception as this single cell starts to divide. This new human being is invisible to the naked eye, no bigger than a pinprick, but already embarked on the course of life.

Within three to four days the fertilized egg travels down the mother's fallopian tube and enters the uterus. The mother's womb has been specially prepared to receive this new life, and by the end of the first week the "ball of life" sinks into the soft, spongy lining of the uterus. Here the embryo begins to develop his own life support system.

Although he receives nourishment from his mother, the unborn child is a genetically unique and biologically separate individual from the time of conception.

*Weeks 3 & 4.* Although only one-fourth inch long, the new baby is rapidly developing. The heart begins to beat between 18 and 25 days after conception, usually before the mother is even aware of her pregnancy. The brain and the spinal column begin to form and the tiny buds that will become arms and legs appear.

*Month 2.* Brain waves can be detected at 40 to 45 days. As the infant grows to an inch or more in length, his facial features become distinct and his tiny skeleton starts to change from cartilage to bone. The child learns to swim freely within the amnionic sac, even though the mother will not likely feel his movement.

By the end of eight weeks the tiny baby looks like a very real person and is completely formed, right down to the unique fingerprints which become his legal identity.

*Month 3.* As the new child grows rapidly he begins to take on distinct qualities of appearance and behavior. Tiny hands and feet are completely developed and his entire body becomes sensitive to touch. All of his body's structures and organs are in place and the baby's nerves and muscles begin to operate.

At just two inches long, the fetus can squint his eyes, swallow, turn his head, curl his toes and make a fist. The baby now sleeps and wakes, he drinks and urinates, and he can feel pain.

*Month 4.* The baby experiences a phenomenal growth spurt during this month, reaching eight to ten inches in height. He sucks his thumb and moves around inside the womb to find a comfortable position for sleep. The baby develops fingernails and hair. His strong heartbeat can be plainly heard as it pumps up to twenty-five quarts of blood each day.

*Months 5 & 6.* The mother feels the baby's movements as he stretches and grows. His sweat and oil glands begin to function. The baby hears his mother's heartbeat and recognizes her voice for the first time. The unborn child leads an active emotional life during this time and his feelings inside the womb begin to shape his attitudes. He can also learn.

The child grows to twelve inches or more and weighs up to one and one-half pounds. Though premature, some infants born at six months can survive with special care.

*Months 7-9.* The child builds up a layer of fat under the skin and develops antibodies for immunity to disease. Each day the infant's heart pumps three hundred gallons of blood and the child absorbs a gallon of amnionic fluid. He triples in weight and grows to about twenty inches.

Consciousness begins about the seventh month. If born at this time, the child will shed tears and cry. About the 30th week the child's neural circuits are complete and there is substantial cerebral functioning. The child is very perceptive to pain and retains memories.

*Birthday.* The mature fetus decides when it is time to be born and signals the placenta. Electro-chemical impulses notify the uterus and the labor contractions begin. The pressure of the uterine muscles propel the baby through the birth canal and out into his new environment.

## Methods of Abortion

*Suction abortion.* Also called vacuum aspiration, this is the most common abortion technique in use today. In this procedure a suction tube is inserted through the dilated cervix into the womb. A powerful vacuum tears the placenta from the uterus and dismembers the body of the developing child, sucking the pieces into an attached jar.

There is a risk that the uterus can be punctured during the procedure. Also, the abortionist must take care that all the body parts are removed from the womb, as infection and hemorrhage can occur if fetal or placental tissue is left in the uterus.

*Dilation and Curettage (D&C).* In a D&C abortion, usually performed between seven and twelve weeks of pregnancy, the doctor inserts a curette, a loop-shaped steel knife, into the womb through the dilated cervix. As the curette scrapes the wall of the uterus, the baby is cut into pieces. Bleeding can be considerable.

As with a suction abortion, there is a risk of infection or hemorrhage, so the abortionist must reassemble the body parts to make sure the uterus is empty.

*Dilation and Evacuation (D&E).* This method is similar to a D&C, except that forceps must be used to grasp the baby's body because of the child's advanced development. The baby is dismembered as the abortionist twists and tears the parts of the body and slices the placenta away from the uterus. Bleeding is profuse.

Although relatively safe for the mother, the procedure is devastating to the hospital staff and many doctors refuse to do advanced D&E abortions.

*Salt Poisoning (Saline Injection).* "Salting out" is the second most common method of inducing abortion and is usually used after sixteen weeks. The doctor inserts a long needle through the mother's abdomen and injects a saline solution into the sac of amnionic fluid surrounding the baby. The baby is poisoned by swallowing the salt and his skin is completely burned away.

It takes about an hour to kill the baby. After the child dies, the mother goes into labor and expels the dead baby. Saline injections have been outlawed in some countries because of the risks to the mother, which can include lung and kidney damage if the salt finds its way into her bloodstream. In spite of the horrible burning effect, some babies have survived "salting out" and been born alive.

*Hysterotomy.* Similar to the Caesarean section, the hysterotomy abortion is a surgical procedure whereby the baby is removed from the mother's womb and allowed to die by neglect or killed by a direct act. This method offers the highest risk to the mother and produces the most number of live births. Hysterotomy is used only for late term pregnancies, and is sometimes used if the salt poisoning or prostaglandin abortion has failed.

*Prostaglandin abortion.* Prostaglandin is a chemical hormone which induces violent labor and premature birth when injected into the amnionic sac. Since prostaglandin results in an unusually high percentage of live births, salt, urea or another toxin is often injected first.

The risk of live birth from a prostaglandin abortion is so great that its use is recommended only in hospitals with neonatal intensive care units. The risk to the mother is also greater with the use of prostaglandin; complications can include cardiac arrest.

RU-486, the so-called "abortion pill," is a prostaglandin drug. Many abortion rights groups advocate the use of this pill as a do-it-yourself abortion method for termination of early pregnancies.

## Arguments and Answers

*There is no way you can stop abortions—women have always had them, and they always will.*

Yes, there will always be abortions, but without legal sanction there would not be as many. Besides, just because an activity happens frequently does not mean that activity should be legalized. Criminals will continue to smuggle drugs no matter how stiff the penalty, but that is no reason to legalize drug trafficking. Should we make rape or murder legal just because we can't stop them from happening?

*We can't go back to the days of "back alley" abortions when so many women died. At least abortion is safe and legal now.*

Abortion proponents have greatly exaggerated the number of deaths due to illegal abortions. Even before *Roe v. Wade* few abortions were self-induced; most, in fact, were performed by licensed physicians. In the decade before abortion was legalized, abortion-related deaths averaged about 225 annually.

Abortion may be legal, but it is not nearly as "safe" as abortion advocates would have us believe. A significant number of women become sterile from botched abortions, or suffer from miscarriages in subsequent pregnancies.

It is difficult to calculate the number of abortion-related deaths in the last few years, since medical records are often changed to protect the privacy of the woman or the reputation of the doctor. Ironically, those who cry loudest to keep abortion "safe and legal" are not interested in regulating abortion clinics where deaths have been reported.

***It's not fair to bring an unwanted child into this world— every child should be wanted.***

This argument is sometimes advanced on behalf of the mother. It is said that no woman should be forced to carry a child she does not want. But an unplanned pregnancy should not be equated with an unwanted child. This argument underrates the ability of mothers to accept their children.

Many women faced with an unplanned pregnancy later report they became satisfied mothers. In any event, once life has begun it is not fair to decide if that life should be continued or destroyed on the basis of convenience to the mother.

At other times this argument is advanced on behalf of the unborn child. It is said that it is unfair to bring an unwanted child into this world, a child doomed to a life of poverty, disease and delinquency.

It is a mark of the degradation of the abortion mentality that the destruction of life can be described as a humane service to the victim. Millions of Americans have overcome economic hardship and even physical handicap to lead happy and fulfilling lives.

Abortion proponents often argue that unwanted children grow up to be the victims of child abuse. Studies show, however, that most abused children are from wanted, or planned pregnancies. It is abortion, not the unwanted child, that is associated with abuse.

Even with the elimination of close to a million and a half unwanted children each year, the incidence of child abuse has risen dramatically since the legalization of abortion. Abortion weakens the social taboo against hurting the helpless and diminishes the value of life.

Finally, there is no such thing as an unwanted child. Millions of couples are waiting to adopt children. There are more than enough loving parents for all the "unwanted" children in the world.

***But aren't the majority of Americans actually in favor of abortion?***

Abortion proponents would like to classify the right to life movement as the work of a small minority, a few vocal fanatics. Since the abortion on demand decision of the Supreme Court has never met with broad public approval, abortion proponents are at pains to provide statistics to support their position.

As a result, surveys are often cited purporting to show that most Americans favor abortion. Most of these polls, however, are based on misleading questions and are designed to elicit a predetermined response.

The truth is that the vast majority of the public is neither adamantly pro-choice or pro-life. When asked whether abortion should be legal in any and all circumstances, fewer than 25% have consistently responded in favor of abortion on demand. Similarly, less than 25% of the public favors a total ban on abortion.

There is, however, a broad consensus on the proper restrictions on abortion. When asked this question, *Do you favor or oppose a ban on all abortions except in the case of rape, incest or when the mother's life is endangered?*, 58% of those polled favored such a ban (*Newsweek*, Jan. 14, 1985).

***What about rape and incest—shouldn't abortion be allowed in these cases?***

Statistically, pregnancy resulting from rape or incest is extremely rare. If pregnancy does occur, the woman's trauma and guilt should not be compounded by the taking of innocent human life. Abortion does not solve the problem of violence or abuse—we should punish the criminal, not the victim.

While not approving of abortion even in the case of rape and incest, many in the pro-life movement are moving towards support of legislation which would allow abortion in those circumstances. This position is considered to be the only viable political reality in light of the fact that the public favors lifting restrictions on abortion in the case of rape and incest. (See the poll cited above.) It is better to save 98% of the unborn children now destroyed by abortion, some pro-life leaders say, than to save none at all.

*What about the woman's right to control her own body?*

The appendix is a part of the woman's own body, an unborn child is not. Although he resides in his mother's womb for nine months, the unborn child is a genetically unique and biologically separate individual.

*Isn't abortion just another form of birth control?*

Birth control, or contraception, is meant to prevent new life from beginning. Abortion destroys life that has already begun.

*Abortion is a religious issue and the government has no business interfering in this private matter.*

The abortion issue crosses all religious and racial lines. It is not a Catholic, or Protestant or Jewish issue. It is not a black, white or brown issue. It is a human life issue, one that goes to the very foundation of our civilization.

Many people without any religious belief whatsoever are opposed to abortion on scientific and moral grounds. For centuries man has held that all life is precious and that the protection of life is a legitimate concern of government. The abortion mentality has rejected this core value of Western society.

*If pro-lifers really cared about life they would work to end poverty and disease and they would empty the orphanages before asking a woman to have an unwanted baby.*

The pro-life movement has often been accused of being indifferent to human needs. But most people active in the right to life movement are also involved in such humanitarian activities as distributing food and clothing to the poor, donating blood, working as volunteers in hospitals, clinics and shelters, and serving as foster and adoptive parents.

In addition to picketing abortion clinics, pro-lifers man crisis pregnancy phone lines, provide financial and material assistance to pregnant women, and many have opened their homes to pregnant women with no place to go. Some 4,000 crisis pregnancy centers across the nation offer alternatives to abortion, including adoption counseling and referral.

## The language of abortion

Realizing that abortion would never be accepted if associated with the idea of killing, proponents of the move to legalize abortion acknowledged early on the necessity of changing the language used in the abortion debate. A fierce campaign of "semantic gymnastics" has been conducted, the success of which can be measured by the *Roe v. Wade* decision and by the way the abortion issue is reported in the news media.

In order to depersonalize the unborn child, the fetus is never referred to as a baby, a child or an infant. In fact, the unborn is rarely even called a fetus. Rather, this new life is called **intra-uterine tissue, the product of conception, potential life, a collection of cells, the conceptus, fetal tissue** or **fetal parts**.

Abortion is never referred to as the taking of human life—how can it be murder when the abortionist is merely performing **a surgical procedure, cleaning out the womb, emptying the uterus,** or **removing foreign tissue from the walls of the uterus**? Killing an unborn child becomes simply the **termination of pregnancy** or **pregnancy interruption, a safe and legal procedure** performed in a **women's health clinic** or a **center for reproductive health**.

Abortion is, of course, **a private decision**, a vital part of a woman's **reproductive freedom**. A woman has a fundamental **right to privacy**, the **right to control her own body**. Abortion proponents are not in favor of murder, they are simply **pro-choice**.

Motherhood, after all, is an **option**.

Amniocentesis allows the doctor to find a **defective fetus** so the pregnancy can be **terminated**. If a handicapped infant manages to escape this search-and-destroy mission, the parents need not be troubled. Infanticide is merely the **withholding of treatment**. And one needn't worry about the aged or infirm becoming a burden—euthanasia is acceptable as **death with dignity**, an **act of mercy**.

# Chapter 2

# Homosexuality and AIDS

Moses said, "I have set before you life and death...therefore choose life, that both thou and thy seed may live" (Deut. 30:19).

For the past 30 years in America, we have been systematically choosing death over life. We have chosen abortion rather than life; we just looked at that issue. We have been choosing death through drug and alcohol abuse.

We have been choosing intellectual death through the lyrics of rock music. We have been choosing death through gang violence.

Now we are endorsing homosexuality, a lifestyle which has spawned the AIDS plague. We're choosing death, not life.

I want to say up front that homosexuality is a sin. We're going to look at that in some detail. But gossiping, lying and backbiting are also sins, and the church gossip and the liar will walk in the same hell with the homosexual. Sin is sin.

That may ruffle the feathers of some sanctimonious birds perched on church pews, but it is the truth. In God's eyes there is no such thing as big sins and little sins.

Let's look at a passage of scripture that describes the foolishness of America.

> Because that, when they knew God, they glorified him
> not as God, neither were thankful; but became vain in
> their imaginations, and their foolish heart was dark-
> ened. Professing themselves to be wise, they became
> fools, And changed the glory of the uncorruptible God
> into an image made like to corruptible man, and to

*birds, and four-footed beasts, and creeping things. Wherefore God also gave them up to uncleanness through the lusts of their own hearts, to dishonor their own bodies between themselves: Who changed the truth of God into a lie, and worshiped and served the creature more than the Creator, who is blessed for ever. Amen. For this cause God gave them up unto vile affections: for even their women did change the natural use into that which is against nature: And likewise also the men, leaving the natural use of the woman, burned in their lust one toward another; men with men working that which is unseemly, and receiving in themselves that recompense of their error which was meet.* Romans 1:21-27

"Professing themselves to be wise, they became fools." That describes America today. They "changed the truth of God into a lie, and worshiped and served the creature more than the Creator." That is a short but accurate definition of the idolatry of secular humanism.

"Receiving in themselves that recompense of their error which was meet." That would certainly include AIDS. The end of that chapter says,

*Who knowing the judgment of God, that they which commit such things are worthy of death, not only do the same, but have pleasure in them that do them.* Romans 1:32

In other words, those who commit these sins know the judgment of God, yet they are not repentant.

## How the Bible describes homosexuality

In the chapter on abortion, we looked at some of the things God hates. Child sacrifice was one of the things listed in Leviticus 18. Also on that list of things God hates is homosexuality.

Verse 22 says, "Thou shalt not lie with mankind, as with womankind; it is abomination."

The Hebrew word translated abomination refers to the absolute worst kind of sin. This is not the only place in the Bible that refers to homosexuality as an abominable sin. In fact, homosexuality is shown to be a capital offense.

> *If a man also lie with mankind, as he lieth with a woman, both of them have committed an abomination: they shall surely be put to death; their blood shall be upon them.* Leviticus 20:13

It is impossible to reconcile scripture with the description of homosexuality as an alternative lifestyle. Homosexuals are demanding recognition socially, politically, and within the church. The Democratic Party has given special recognition to homosexuals in the gay rights plank of their platform.

Some churches are ordaining homosexuals to preach and approving their lifestyle from the pulpit. Other churches are standing against homosexuality as an abomination unto God. Who is right? What does God's word say?

As we have seen, God's word addresses the question specifically. If you believe the Bible is God's word and that it is true, you cannot recognize homosexuality as a legitimate lifestyle.

If you want to know why humanists hate the word of God, here it is in a nutshell. The word of God establishes the standard of righteousness. It establishes absolutes—moral, spiritual and social. Humanists do not want anyone telling them what is right and wrong. They don't want anyone—God, the church or anyone else—suggesting there is no basis for their "if it feels right, do it" philosophy.

I am telling you that the word of God was here before we got here, and it will be here long after we're gone, if God tarries. The Bible is the truth—it is not trying to the be truth, it is truth. Every man who falls upon the word of God will be broken, but upon whomever it falls, it will grind him to powder (Matt. 21:44).

Phil Donohue likes to joyously announce on his television program that the word "homosexual" is not found in scripture. He is absolutely right. The word "homosexual" is nowhere found in scripture.

The author of the scripture, the Holy Spirit, knew that people of varying degrees of education would read this book. So it is written in word pictures so unmistakably clear that anyone can grasp it: "If a man also lie with mankind, as he lieth with a woman, both of them have committed an abomination." If you have the intelligence quotient of a fresh water trout, you can recognize that as an accurate definition of homosexuality.

So what does the Bible call homosexuality? An abomination. That means something disgusting and abhorrent, the strongest word the Bible uses to describe sin. Homosexuality is rebellion against the established order of God. It says that in no uncertain terms both in the Old Testament, and in the New Testament.

## God's urban renewal program for Sodom

Let me pose a question. Will homosexuals be satisfied with recognition by politicians and the churches, or will they become even more aggressive? There is a case study of homosexuality in the 19th chapter of Genesis which will answer this question. We get our English word sodomy, defined as "copulation with a member of the same sex or with an animal," from this passage of scripture describing the sin of the city of Sodom.

> *And there came two angels to Sodom at even; and Lot sat in the gate of Sodom: and Lot seeing them rose up to meet them; and he bowed himself with his face toward the ground; And he said, Behold now, my lords, turn in, I pray you, into your servant's house, and tarry all night, and wash your feet, and ye shall rise up early, and go on your ways. And they said, Nay; but we will abide in the street all night. And he pressed upon them greatly; and they turned in unto him, and entered into his house; and he made them a feast, and did bake unleavened bread, and they did eat.*
> *But before they lay down, the men of the city, even the men of Sodom, compassed the house round, both*

*old and young, all the people from every quarter: And*
*they called unto Lot, and said unto him, Where are the*
*men which came in to thee this night? bring them out*
*unto us, that we may know them.* Genesis 19:1-5

This is a public demonstration coming against Lot. They knew
Lot had guests in his house, and they called them men. They
wanted to "know them," which means to have sexual intercourse
with them.

*And Lot went out at the door unto them, and shut the*
*door after him, And said, I pray you, brethren, do not*
*so wickedly. Behold now, I have two daughters which*
*have not known man; let me, I pray you, bring them out*
*unto you, and do ye to them as is good in your eyes:*
*only unto these men do nothing; for therefore came*
*they under the shadow of my roof.* Genesis 19:6-8

Lot told them, "do not so wickedly." In other words, do not
behave yourselves as Sodomites. Lot was a wimp who offered
his own daughters to these men. Knowing they were homosexuals,
he figured they would not bother the women. He knew what they
really wanted were the men in his house.

*And they said, Stand back. And they said again, This*
*one fellow came in to sojourn, and he will needs be a*
*judge: now will we deal worse with thee, than with*
*them. And they pressed sore upon the man, even Lot,*
*and came near to break the door.* Genesis 19:9

Now they're threatening to sexually abuse Lot, and trying to
destroy his property.

*But the men put forth their hand, and pulled Lot into*
*the house to them, and shut to the door. And they smote*
*the men that were at the door of the house with*
*blindness, both small and great: so that they wearied*
*themselves to find the door.* Genesis 19:10-11

The Sodomites didn't repent when they were struck with
blindness, they just scrambled for the door.

There are several important lessons we need to learn here. First of all, this was a public demonstration intended to intimidate Lot into surrendering his house guests to them for sexual purposes. That's what you call aggressive and out of the closet. They came from every part of the city—it was the original Gay Pride Day. They circled the house, both young and old. These were not closet homosexuals, this was a pattern of behavior. They were as aggressive as a pack of wolves.

They were willing to disregard Lot's property rights. They tried to break down the door and violate the integrity of his home because of their sexual lust for the men inside. They made threats when they did not get their way. Then the judgment of God came on them by the angels striking them with blindness.

Now if you think God tolerates homosexuality, just consider his urban renewal program for Sodom and Gomorrah. It's right there in Genesis 19.

I say this to every nation in the world that openly endorses homosexuality: the judgment of God will come to your nation. That is a guarantee. America's number one problem right now is God, because God will not tolerate sin.

God judges sin and he judges it speedily in the fierceness of his wrath. The only thing that matches the love of God is the wrath of God. If you don't know anything about the wrath of God, read up on it. America is about to experience it.

## The homosexual challenge to Christianity

Congressman William Dannemeyer of California has written a book called **Shadow In The Land**. The following quote is from pages 106-107 of his book, where he outlines the homosexual challenge to the Christians of America.

> *As for Jesus, He never said a word of condemnation against homosexuality, a fact that indicates that He didn't really see anything wrong with such attachments.*[1]

Dannemeyer is paraphrasing the militant homosexuals here.

This is obviously not a correct statement. Jesus did not mention the word rape, either. But that doesn't mean he condoned it.

*Relying on these isolated statements in the Bible, as well as an ongoing tradition of bigotry, Jews and Christians have been homophobes for the better part of 3,000 years, persecuting homosexuals more than any other minority in the history of Western civilization.*[2]

That's another untrue statement, and I will address the issue of homosexuals as a minority further on in this chapter.

*But now the tide has turned. We have at last 'come out,' and in so doing we have exposed the mean-spirited nature of Judeo-Christian morality. You have been narrow-minded and self-righteous. But with the help of a growing number of your own membership, we are going to force you to recant everything you have ever believed or said about sexuality. Here are some of the things you will be expected to affirm, in the process of renouncing love, marriage, and family:*

*(1) Henceforth homosexuality will be spoken of in your churches and synagogues as an 'honorable estate.'*

*(2) You can either let us marry people of the same sex or better yet abolish marriage altogether, since it will give the lie to everything you have said and done in the past about sexuality.*

*(3) You will also be expected to offer ceremonies that bless our sexual arrangements, whether or not you retain marriage as something to be celebrated in your churches.*

*(4) You will also instruct your young people in homosexual as well as heterosexual behavior, and you will go out of your way to make certain that homosexual youths are allowed to date, attend religious functions together, openly display affection, and enjoy each*

*other's sexuality without embarrassment or guilt.*

*(5) If any of the older people in your midst object, you will deal with them sternly, making certain they renounce their ugly and ignorant homophobia or suffer public humiliation.*

*(6) You will also make certain that all of the prestige and resources of your institutions are brought to bear on the community, so that laws are passed forbidding discrimination against homosexuals and heavy punishments are assessed. We expect and demand the same commitment to us that you made to blacks and to women, though their suffering has not been as great as ours.*

*(7) Finally, we will in all likelihood want to expunge a number of passages from your Scriptures and rewrite others, eliminating preferential treatment of marriage and using words that will allow for homosexual interpretations of passages describing biblical lovers such as Ruth and Boaz or Solomon and the Queen of Sheba.*

**Warning:** *If all of these things do not come to pass quickly, we will subject orthodox Jews and Christians to the most sustained hatred and vilification in recent memory. We have captured the liberal establishment and the press. We have already beaten you on a number of battlefields. And we have the spirit of the age on our side. You have neither the faith nor the strength to fight us, so you might as well surrender now.*[3]

These are the demands of the homosexuals to the church in America, ladies and gentlemen. They are at the door and they are trying to knock it down. If those statements aren't threats, I don't know what they are.

Already many municipalities have passed laws forbidding discrimination against homosexuals. Some of these laws have taken the form of stiff civil and criminal penalties for so-called "hate crimes." Politicians have taken the very just laws which prohibit discrimination against any person on the basis of race, creed or color, and added the phrase "sexual preference."

The inclusion of those two words in anti-discrimination laws will be used in attempt to stop preachers from preaching that homosexuality is an abomination to God. They want preachers who preach that from the pulpit to spend the night in jail.

Let me say something here about what is called "gay bashing" in the press. Homosexuals want to make it a crime to say anything against homosexuality. That goes against freedom of speech and freedom of religion. They also want to pass these hate crime laws to enforce stiff criminal penalties against thugs who attack and beat up homosexuals simply because they are homosexual.

As to the first point, I can assure you that hell will freeze over and I'll skate on the ice before I ever stop preaching that homosexuality is a sin. But as to the second point, absolutely nothing in the word of God sanctions assault and battery against homosexuals simply because homosexuality is a sin.

So while I will continue to preach that homosexuality is an abomination to God, I do not condone physical violence against homosexuals. We have laws already on the books that make violence against homosexuals a crime. They are the same assault and battery laws that protect all of us from physical violence. We do not need to make "gay bashing" a "hate crime" in order to prosecute physical attacks on homosexuals. We need to enforce the laws we already have, and Christians need to speak out *for* righteousness and *against* violence.

Not only have some cities passed anti-discrimination laws, some colleges are offering sanction of and protection for homosexuals and homosexual groups on campus. Rutgers, the State University of New Jersey, is a prime example. The following quote is from the February 3, 1992 edition of the *Wall Street Journal* in an article titled, "Gay Students Enjoy Programs, Protections At Rutgers University."

> *During "Coming Out Days," gay and lesbian students have a "kiss-in" on Brower Commons, across from*

*the student center. And under the university's contro-*
*versial anti-insult policy, homosexuals don't have to*
*suffer slurs in silence, any more than blacks or Jews*
*must endure epithets on campus. The policy forbids*
*even "belittling comments." Break the rules and you*
*may have to clean toilets.*

*In the dorms, Rutgers students can request and be*
*assigned a gay roommate as casually as they might*
*request a non-smoker...Rutgers now offers benefits to*
*"bona fide sole domestic partners" of gay faculty*
*members...*

*The enemy is no longer merely the "homophobe"*
*(one who fears or hates homosexuals), but also the*
*"heterosexist" (a coinage denoting one who believes*
*that heterosexuality is preferable to homosexuality).*
*Gay authors and themes have been introduced into*
*half a dozen academic disciplines, and the women's*
*studies department offers a lecture series called*
*"Beyond Heterosexism." The university also provides*
*sensitivity training to freshmen and shows a video*
*about the gay community, "A Little Respect." And the*
*Rutgers art school played host to a show by lesbian*
*and gay artists titled "Outrageous Desires."*

Homosexuals are trying to get their status recognized as a
politically-protected minority. Homosexuality is not a minority
group like women or blacks or Hispanics. Homosexuality is a
choice. You do not have a choice whether you are born male or
female, black or white or brown. You are not born homosexual,
however; homosexuality is a learned behavior. We will look at
the medical proof of that further in this chapter.

## Homosexuality and AIDS

Homosexuals and intravenous drug users brought AIDS to
America. But understand that AIDS is no longer a homosexual
problem. AIDS is a problem to every man, woman, boy and girl

who wants to live.

Dr. Robert Strecker of Los Angeles, who is both an MD and a PhD, says these fives things about AIDS:

(1) AIDS is not a homosexual disease;

(2) AIDS is not a venereal disease;

(3) AIDS can be carried by mosquitoes;

(4) condoms will not prevent AIDS;

(5) there can never be a vaccine against the AIDS virus.[4]

He also says that the "miracle drug" AZT is nothing but junk food for the AIDS virus.

Although decades have passed and untold billions have been spent on cancer research, it is still with us. Dr. Strecker, who specializes in the treatment of AIDS and cancer, says that the most dreaded fear of oncologists (cancer specialists) is the idea that some day cancer will be able to be transmitted from one person to the other, that it will become contagious and transferrable. AIDS has made that nightmare a reality.

Dr. Haseltine of Harvard University says, "the AIDS virus is species threatening."[5] Don't you love the way academics talk? What he means is that AIDS has the potential to exterminate every human being on planet Earth.

We are being comforted with an array of numbers that pour out of our resource centers trying to give us the picture that everything is okay and the number of new AIDS cases is dwindling. Well, the data that say the number of AIDS cases is leveling off came out of San Francisco, and is meant to give the impression that AIDS is on the run.

But the reason the number of new AIDS cases is leveling off in San Francisco, is that when the number reaches the saturation point, it can't get any higher. In other words, 100% is 100%. When you reach 100%, how can there be any new cases? There has to be a leveling off at the saturation point.

Dr. William Campbell Douglas says,

*If you believe the government propaganda that AIDS is hard to catch, then you are going to die even sooner than the rest of us.*

*The common cold is a virus. Have you ever had a cold? How did you catch it? You don't really know, do you?*

*If the cold virus were fatal, how many people would be left in the world?*

*Yellow fever is a virus. You catch it from mosquito bites. Malaria is a parasite also carried by mosquitoes. It is many times larger than the AIDS virus (like comparing a pinhead to a moose head), yet the mosquito easily carries this large organism to man.*[6]

Now if mosquitoes can carry AIDS (and a number of medical sources say they definitely can), and *not* transmit AIDS to man, then science owes it to humanity to find out what it is in the mosquito that filters AIDS out.

## The myth of "safe sex"

Not only are we getting questionable information from the medical community, we are getting absolutely the wrong message from the government and liberal media. All we have heard recently from politicians, educators, psychologists and commentators is "Safe sex, safe sex, safe sex. Pass out the condoms and save America."

If it weren't so sad, it would be hysterically funny.

We have spent trillions of dollars on national defense. Missiles that can be guided by electronic beams through the air. AWACS. Radar-evading Stealth bombers. Technology so sophisticated that if a rat rolls his eyes in the basement of the Kremlin, we know which direction he was looking.

But now that we're facing a plague that could literally wipe out our population, we're coming out with a new national defense program: a twenty-five cent condom. Doesn't that make you feel absolutely *safe*?

Let me tell you something you already know: condoms will not save America. The only thing that will save America is repentance and morality.

"Safe sex" is a slogan for morons. We tell our children, "Don't drink and drive, it'll kill you." We tell them, "Say no to drugs, they'll kill you." But what do we tell them about sex? We tell them it's safe. Just use a condom and you'll be okay.

We are what the Bible calls fools. The message America needs to hear is not the message of "safe sex." The message America needs to hear is the message of abstinence, repentance and purity. We need to hear the message of holiness, "without which no man shall see the Lord" (Heb. 12:14).

The Bible says "the wages of sin is death" (Rom. 6:23), and "the soul that sinneth, it shall die" (Ezek. 18:20). There is a payday someday. There is a high price for low living. Your choices have consequences.

The sexual laws of God's word are not meant to harass you and make you feel socially obsolete. They are meant to save your life. Those around you may say, "Let's party. This is the way to really live." But they are fools racing toward the graveyard. "There is a way that seemeth right unto a man; but the end thereof are the ways of death" (Prov. 16:25). Live by the purity of the word of God and you will have happiness and health.

Sex is wonderful. God invented it. Most of you are here because of it! But "safe sex" is not a matter of how well you master the use of a condom. "Safe sex," according to God's word, is sex between one man and one woman married to each other for life. That's what "safe sex" is all about.

This is the time to speak out or be what Isaiah called "a dumb dog."

> [The Lord's] *watchmen are all blind: they are all ignorant, they are all dumb dogs, they cannot bark; sleeping, lying down, loving to slumber.* Isaiah 56:10

Isaiah said that in an hour of crisis the Lord's watchmen were dumb dogs who could not bark, that is, they could not announce danger. Unfortunately that describes most of America's clergy.

I would rather be hated by the world and labeled by the humanistic, leftist, liberal press as a redneck, fundamentalist evangelical than to stand before God on the day of judgment and have him say, "You knew the truth but you didn't speak it. You were a dumb dog. In the day of danger you kept your mouth shut and you let people stumble into the abyss of disease and hell without ever warning them."

## The impact of AIDS

We keep hearing that the AIDS virus is very fragile and you can't catch AIDS from casual contact. Just how fragile and delicate is the AIDS virus? Dr. James Schlaff of the National Institute of Health says that the AIDS virus can live outside the body for several days. Now doesn't that sound fragile! The British medical journal LANCET reported on September 8, 1985 that the virus can live for a week in a culture dish. The Pasteur Institute of France states the virus can live for fifteen days outside the body at room temperature. So if someone coughs, the virus can stay in the room, lying dormant for up to two weeks. Yes sir, that's a fragile virus.

If you cannot get AIDS through casual contact, then why do doctors who treat AIDS patients look more like Robocop than Dr. Kildare? Rock Hudson died in one of the best hospitals in the world, an institution with a history of AIDS treatment. Every doctor and nurse who touched Rock Hudson was wearing two sets of gloves, a mask, and disposable gowns and shoes. When they left the room, their protective gear was removed and burned. So why did they go to all that trouble if the AIDS virus is so fragile?

The answer is that medical science is not even sure what they know about AIDS. And if they told America what they do know about AIDS, pandemonium might break out. Americans might get so moved they would get up off their duffs and demand their politicians do something to protect them. They would demand that doctors with AIDS not be permitted to practice. They would demand that property owners not be forced to rent their property to someone who is infected with AIDS, and that employers not be forced to hire AIDS carriers.

The number of AIDS cases is supposed to increase by 600% by 1995. That means nine million cases of AIDS in America and a million deaths, mostly to the youth of our country, the flower and hope of the nation.

By the year 2000, twenty million Americans will have AIDS. One in every ten people in our schools, our offices and our churches will be a diseased, infected time bomb.

Enrollment in private schools is exploding, even in our currently depressed economy. Why? Parents are seeking a safe environment for their children's education. Thanks to the ACLU and homosexual political action committees, both of which are well organized and highly funded, AIDS testing will not be done in public schools because it is an "invasion of privacy." But AIDS testing can be done in private schools, and more of them will be requiring it.

Think of it. In eight short years, one in ten children in public schools will have the AIDS virus. That will make the public school the most dangerous place you can send your child. A schoolyard accident or a sports injury could mean the death of your child.

## The wrong role models

Not all AIDS comes from sexual activity, but most does. Many people who have AIDS have led a clean, straight life. AIDS has now become so pervasive that there's not a person reading this who is not susceptible, even if you are living a pure life.

Young people need to know that it only takes one sexual relationship with an HIV carrier to kill you. Teenage girls, when you go to bed with Jimmy to "prove your love" (and what an idiotic expression that is), you are not going to bed with just Jimmy—you are going to bed with everybody Jimmy ever went to bed with and everybody they ever went to bed with. You may be going to bed with hundreds or thousands of people.

Basketball star Wilt Chamberlain recently published a book in which he admitted to 20,000 adulterous relationships with 1,000 different women during his NBA career. Frankly, I think he's lying through his teeth. You don't have to be a rocket scientist to put that in a computer and figure out that he could not have gotten out of bed long enough to play a game if all that's true.

But that's the kind of role model America's young people are looking up to. That's the wrong role model. Our role model is not some over-sexed, egotistical basketball star, rock star or movie star. Our role model is Jesus Christ, the Son of the living God. When you stand before God on Judgment Day we will be judged by the standard of righteousness found in the word of God, not the standard of morality of Playboy, Madonna or some nymphomaniac out of the NBA.

AIDS is the fourth largest killer in America right now. In Nigeria, 80% of the professionals have AIDS, 85% of the military have AIDS, and 99% of the prisoners have AIDS. Perhaps you think, well, that's because it started over in Africa. Maybe so, but now it's here. And there's no known cure. Some doctors say there never will be a cure.

Politicians are saying that if we can get the American people to give us billions of dollars for research, we might find a solution that works for some people in 20 years. I know a cure for AIDS that will stop the epidemic in one generation. It will not cost one dime, and I guarantee its success. It will drive the AIDS virus from the bloodstream of every American. The cure for AIDS is purity. Let's try that for a while.

The Bible says that the days before the Lord's return will be as it was in the days of Noah and in the days of Lot (Luke 17:26-30). What was it like in those days? First, there was excessive materialism and greed; we certainly qualify on that count.

Secondly, there was eating and drinking, which means they were a gluttonous society. America is a hedonistic society, living only for the gratification of the self. Lastly, there was an aggressive homosexual community, which I have already described.

## It couldn't happen in America...

Consider the past thirty years in America. Thirty years ago, no one thought much about homosexuality or what is now called "gay rights." There were no Gay Pride parades with men passionately kissing each other while walking down Broadway, some dressed like women, taunting the citizens with sexual slurs and hand signals for all the television cameras to see.

Thirty years ago politicians were not tripping all over themselves to publicly announce their support for gay rights, as did every Democratic presidential candidate in 1988 and the present platform of the Democratic party. Today the news media and liberal politicians are bombarding America with the demand for homosexual rights. Congress is being pressured to pass a "gay rights bill."

Let me ask a question: where did they ever get the insane idea that there is a right to sodomize? They didn't get it from the word of God. We've already looked at what the Bible has to say about so-called homosexual rights. They didn't get it from the Constitution, either.

Congressman Dannemeyer says,

> *The gay rights bill will include the right for homosexuals to marry and the right to adopt children. Every business will be put on notice that homosexuals must be hired regardless of the moral or religious convictions of the employer. School sex education will be revised to depict sodomy as normal...*
>
> *Teachers will be hired who approve of homosexual rights and who are homosexuals themselves, to make sure there is no discrimination. Homosexual clubs will be in every school, as presently exists in Los Angeles. Even church schools who receive government money will be forced to subsidize homosexual activities on the campus, which has already happened at Georgetown University.*[7]

In that situation, the government forced Georgetown University, a Catholic university, to recognize a homosexual club and give it carte blanche on campus. It would have been a great hour for the Catholic church if they would have closed down the school and said they weren't going to have it. But they capitulated to the government, which is what most people do.

People say this could never happen in America. Wake up! It's already happening. People were saying that about prayer in schools just twenty years ago. People were saying that about abortion just twenty years ago.

What can you do about it?

The first thing you can do is open your Bible and find out that homosexuality is an abomination to God. It is not now, nor will it ever be, an alternative lifestyle acceptable to anybody but the devil himself.

Secondly, you can quit being a political couch potato and get up off your backside, get registered to vote, and vote against every Congressman, Senator and Presidential candidate who is for the gay rights bill.

## Homosexuality: choice or chance?

Homosexuals attempt to justify their sin on the basis of genetics. They say they are born homosexuals and can't help themselves. That's a bald-faced lie. It is not medically true. The only medical support for that thesis comes from the people they hired to do research projects and from the liberal media practicing Hitler's methodology of telling a lie often enough and big enough until most of the mindless citizens believe it.

Contrary to homosexual belief, God did not make them that way. "Let no man say when he is tempted, I am tempted of God: for God cannot be tempted with evil, neither tempteth he any man" (James 1:13). God did not put within you a poison pill called sodomy, which will destroy your body and your soul. Sin and death do not come from God. They come from Satan, the prince of darkness, who is out to rob you, kill you and destroy you.

Medical evidence overwhelmingly supports the position that homosexuality is derived by choice, that is, by learning and conditioning, not by chance. Wainwright Churchill, in his study **Homosexual Behavior Among Males** states, "There is no sexual instinct in man. Human sexuality is entirely dependent upon learning and conditioning."[8] Dr. Robert Frumkin, in his **Encyclopedia of Sexual Behavior** states, "There is no sexual instinct in man." [9]

Masters and Johnson, who are certainly not charismatics, say in their study **Human Sexuality**, "The genetic theory of homosexuality has been generally discarded today."[10] There are other blue ribbon medical studies that support the fact that homosexuality is learned behavior. It is determined by choice, not chance.

The bottom line is this: you are morally responsible for your conduct. Choices have consequences.

Suppose for a moment that you buy the absurd logic of the homosexuals, "It's in my genes and I can't help it." Carry that logic further. "My parents had a bad temper and so do I. It's in my genes. I just get mad and kill people. I can't help it." On the basis of that logic, we should let all the serial killers out of the penitentiaries, since they were born that way and can't help themselves. That's where that logic takes you. But in truth, you are responsible for your actions.

"My mother was a kleptomaniac. She loved to steal and so do I. If it's not nailed down, I'll take it; and if it is, I'll lay down beside it and claim it. I can't help it. It's in my genes." No, you are responsible for your actions.

From the Garden of Eden, man has been playing the blame game. When Adam sinned he said to God, "This woman that you gave me—she made me do it." People are still using that argument today. Flip Wilson used to say, "The devil made me do it." We blame things on demons that embarrass the devil himself. We blame the stars. "It's written in the stars." We blame our parents and we blame society. That's good freshman psychology, but it's terrible theology.

The Bible says that when we come to Christ, we become new creatures. "Old things are passed away; behold all things are become new" (2 Cor. 5:17). We have new friends, we have new habits, we have new attitudes. We have a new heart, a new mind, a new body, and a new name written down in glory.

You can be a new person by living by the word of God. Stop wading around in the sewer of your past blaming your sad, sorry, sin-sick life on someone else. You are responsible for what you are.

Our young people need to start getting moral instruction from the church and synagogue rather than movie stars and rock stars. America's society is sick. This is not a Great Society, it is a sick society.

TV sitcoms are sick; if they're not sick, they're intellectually bankrupt, which is another way of saying they're stupid. Authors are sick, porno videos are sick, rock stars are sick, most movies are sick and most magazines are sick. They are written by sick, twisted, depraved, lost, humanistic pagans who hate God, hate God's word and hate moral absolutes. Their words maim, cripple, injure and kill. They have no place in your life—throw them out. Stop getting your instruction from Norman Lear and Madonna. Get your instruction from Moses and Jesus Christ. They've got the answer.

You have a choice: repentance or exposure. Proverbs 28:13 says, "He that covereth his sins shall not prosper: but whoso confesseth and forsaketh them shall have mercy." That's your option.

Romans 1:22 says, "Professing themselves to be wise, they became fools." That describes America. 1 Corinthians 1:20 says that the wisdom or philosophy of this world is just so much foolishness with God. We are seeing the last-days decadence and the death of the nation. The Bible says that we will see earthquakes, famines and pestilences in various places in the last days (Luke 21:11). A pestilence is a disease with no cure. That's AIDS.

The good news is that the blood of Jesus Christ cleanses from all sin.

*If we confess our sins, he is faithful and just to forgive us our sins, and to cleanse us from all unrighteousness.*
1 John 1:9

God loves every homosexual. But he does not accept homosexuality. He will forgive the sin of homosexuality if you will ask him. If you want to change and follow Jesus, we'll endorse you.

We minister to homosexuals in our church. We pray for those with AIDS. We counsel those trapped in the bondage of homosexuality and we have support groups for recovering homosexuals.

But understand where the line is drawn. We will not now, nor will we ever, accept homosexuality as an alternative lifestyle, because God's word says it is an abomination. That's the bottom line. We choose to live by God's laws and not society's suggestions.

## Notes

1. Dannemeyer, William. *Shadow In The Land.* (San Francisco: Ignatius Press, 1989), p. 106.

2. *ibid*, p. 106.

3. *ibid*, p. 106-107, emphasis added.

4. Strecker, Robert B., MD, PhD. *The Strecker Memorandum.* (VHS video: 1216 Wilshire Blvd., Los Angeles, CA 90017).

5. Antonio, Gene. *The AIDS Cover-Up.* (San Francisco: Ignatius Press, 1987)

6. Douglass, William Campbell, M.D. *Spotlight,* Nov. 23, 1987.

7. Dannemeyer, p. 85-86

8. Churchill, Wainwright. *Homosexual Behavior Among Males.* (New York: 1967), p. 101.

9. Frumkin, Robert. *The Encyclopedia of Sexual Behavior.* (New York: 1967), p. 439.

10. Masters, William H.; Brown, Virginia E.; and Kolodny, Robert C. *Human Sexuality.* (Boston: 1984), p. 319

## Chapter 3

# The Feminist Movement

No book in the history of the world champions the cause of women more than the Bible. "Who can find a virtuous woman? For her price is far above rubies" (Prov. 31:10).

St. Paul said, "Husbands, love your wives, even as Christ also loved the church, and gave himself for it" (Eph. 5:25). That was one of the most radical statements ever made about women's rights, made at a point in history when women were considered part of a man's ownership, like his cattle.

We are considering now the feminist war in America. I am not referring to women who have genuine concerns that affect the quality of life. There are far too many women in our country who are abused by their husbands who batter them, by their employers who refuse to give them equal pay for equal work, and by men in the work force who sexually harass them.

That should not happen, but it does. And these women need help from the church to recapture their self-esteem after being battered, and help from the government to guarantee that they are compensated properly for their work, and protected from the macho male with the mentality that it is his right to speak or touch in a sexually offensive manner.

The Bible does not support the abuse of or discrimination against women in any way. There is true equality in Jesus Christ. "There is neither Jew nor Greek, there is neither bond nor free, there is neither male nor female: for ye are all one in Christ Jesus" (Gal. 3:28).

So when I speak of the feminist movement, I am not speaking of the genuine concerns of women for equality and respect.

I am speaking of a rapidly growing feminist movement whose objective is to control the government through intimidation and to restructure the traditional family by removing the male as the leader. I am speaking of a radical group who is attacking the church, especially the Bible-preaching church, with an agenda promoting occult worship, specifically the worship of the goddess the Bible calls Ashteroth. I am speaking of a group who, in their words, has "rediscovered the power of witchcraft" and is disseminating that belief to millions of women in the feminist movement.

There is a wealth of writings by this rapidly growing radical movement, as a trip to your local bookstore will evidence. I am going to quote here from a sampling of feminist writings. These and other books are the cornerstone of philosophy for this radical feminist movement.

## The spiritual dimension of the feminist movement

Feminist/pagan writer (her designation) Starhawk said, in an address delivered in 1977 to the American Academy of Religion:

> *The feminist movement, which began as a political, economic, and social struggle, is opening to a spiritual dimension. In the process, many women are discovering the old religion, reclaiming the word* witch *and, with it, some of our lost culture.*[1]

Feminist Barbara Ardinger proudly announces, "As a visit to your local bookstore will show, there's a whole library of Goddess books already on the shelves and more on the way."[2] Understand that the goddess she refers to is a female god figure which many feminists worship.

Why has the feminist movement left the political realm and entered the realm of religion? Carol Christ says,

> *Because religion has such a compelling hold on the deep psyches of so many people, feminists cannot afford to leave it in the hands of the fathers. Even people who no longer 'believe in God' or participate in the institutional structure of patriarchal religion still may not be free of the power of the symbolism of God the Father.[3]*

This is a radical attack on the church and the leadership of God. This attack is spelled out by Mary Daly in her essay *After the Death of God the Father: Women's Liberation and the Transformation of Christian Consciousness.*

> *As the women's revolution begins to have its effect upon the fabric of society, transforming it from patriarchy into something that never existed before...it will become the greatest single potential challenge to Christianity to rid itself of its oppressive tendencies or go out of business.[4]*

Daly refers to male leadership as "oppressive tendencies." Her intent is to rid the church of these oppressive tendencies, or make it go out of business. That sounds like a threat to me.

## Rebellion against God is witchcraft

The feminist movement in America is about the spirit of rebellion against God's plan for the family. The Bible equates this spirit of rebellion with witchcraft. 1 Samuel 15:23 states it very plainly: "For rebellion is as the sin of witchcraft."

Many of the feminist writers openly admit they are promoting witchcraft. In the address previously quoted, Starhawk also says:

> *Witchcraft, 'the craft of the wise,' is the last remnant in the west of the time of women's strength and power. Through the dark ages of persecution, the covens of Europe preserved what is left of the mythology, rituals, and knowledge of the ancient matricentric (mother-*

*centered) times...But [witch]craft remains, in spite of*
*all efforts to stamp it out, as a living tradition of*
*Goddess-centered worship that traces its roots back to*
*the time before the triumph of patriarchy.*[5]

In other words, witchcraft goes back beyond the time of leadership of men, "the triumph of patriarchy," to a time when the world was controlled by women through the spirit of witchcraft. Let me give you the Hagee translation of what Starhawk is saying: "Women of America, rise up and with a spirit of witchcraft throw off any control of God the Father, throw off any plan of male leadership, and rise to become the power within yourself."

The objective of feminism is the destruction of masculine leadership in the home, the church and the government. I believe it is Rush Limbaugh who refers to this movement as the "femi-Nazi movement," and that's probably a good description.

This radical feminist group wants to control our government through threat and manipulation, to attack the Bible-believing church, and to bring witchcraft and the occult, specifically goddess worship, to the women of America.

## Who is the goddess they worship?

Many of the feminist writings refer to goddess worship. I should point out that some feminists worship many goddesses, and some do not believe that the goddesses are real, but merely "psychological archetypes."

Yet many feminists refer to a Mother Goddess or Great Goddess as the ancestral spirit of their religion. When you dig far enough into their philosophy, you will find that the Great Goddess to whom they refer is the goddess the Bible calls Ashteroth.

One of the important writings in this line of feminist thinking is **When God Was A Woman** by Merlin Stone. She describes her search for the goddess this way:

> *In the beginning, people prayed to the Creatress of*
> *Life, the Mistress of Heaven. At the very dawn of*
> *religion, God was a woman. Do you remember?...*
>
> *For years, something has magnetically lured me*
> *into exploring the legends, the temple sites, the stat-*
> *ues, and the ancient rituals of the female deities,*
> *drawing me back in time to an age when the Goddess*
> *was omnipotent, and women acted as Her clergy,*
> *controlling the form and rites of religion.[6]*

I can tell you that the "something" that "magnetically lured"
Ms. Stone into goddess worship was in reality an evil spirit. It is
the spirit of Lucifer, or Satan, who rebelled against God's
authority and was thrown out of heaven.

She goes on to identify the goddess she discovered:

> *It was not long before the various pieces of evidence*
> *fell into place and the connections began to take form.*
> *And then I understood. Ashtoreth, the despised 'pagan'*
> *deity of the Old Testament was...actually Astarte—the*
> *Great Goddess...elsewhere known as...Asherah...—*
> *the many-named Divine Ancestress.[7]*

Who is Ashtoreth, the female deity worshipped by Merlin
Stone and other feminists?

Ashtoreth, the most hated occult goddess of the Old Testament, was worshipped by Jezebel, who was a witch and who
controlled the government of Israel through manipulation and
intimidation of her spineless husband, King Ahab. Jezebel
opposed and persecuted the prophets of Israel, including Elijah.
(See 1 Kings 18-21 and 2 Kings 9.)

Ashtoreth was a Canaanite fertility goddess, the female
counterpart of Baal. She was worshiped in what the Bible calls
the "high places," groves on a hill centered around poles with
images of a many-breasted woman carved at the top. The "high
places" were gathering places for those given to complete
depravity: sexual orgies, homosexual and heterosexual prostitution, sex with animals, and all manner of deviate sexual
behavior.

Even King Solomon was seduced into the worship of Ashteroth by his foreign wives (1 Kings 11:5-8). King Josiah, known as a reformer, was commended for tearing down the high places of Ashteroth worship (2 Kings 23:13-14, 19-20).

Every time Israel as a nation worshipped Ashtoreth, which was three different times, God cut them off. On one occasion God said to Israel, "You are no longer my people." In the most brutal of terms, God separated himself from them.

How did God react to the worship of Ashtoreth? He sent Israel into captivity. Their women were raped. Their children were murdered before their eyes. They were enslaved. They lived in hunger and mind-bending poverty after the collapse of their economy. This is God's judgment on goddess worship.

That radical feminists want to bring the worship of Ashtoreth to the women of America should drive Bible-believing Christians to their knees. The word of God must be preached from the pulpits of America, and on television, and by every means possible, until the sincere women in this nation who have legitimate complaints recognize there is a better venue through which to express their complaints and redress their grievances than through the feminist movement.

This is the time for the church of Jesus Christ to turn on the light of the gospel. The answer for America is the word of God. That is the only thing than can bring this nation back from the brink of moral disaster.

This is a decade of decision. If the church does not rise up and preach the power of the word of God, in ten years we will bequeath to our children a nation that is beyond the brink. It is time for Christians to rise up and speak up. The Bible says, "Let the redeemed of the Lord say so."

It is time for the church of Jesus Christ to come to order and begin to express their Bible convictions. It is time for every Christian to say, "I believe that Jesus Christ is Lord. I believe the Bible is the truth. I stand upon the authority of the word of God and I will not be intimidated, I will not be manipulated and I will not be dominated."

## Manifestation of the feminist attack

In her essay *Why Women Need the Goddess: Phenomeno-logical, Psychological, and Political Reflections,* Carol Christ says:

> *Religions centered on the worship of a male God create 'moods' and 'motivations' that keep women in a state of psychological dependence on men and male authority, while at the same legitimating the* political *and* social *authority of fathers and sons in the institutions of society.*[8]

She is saying that a religion which gives the place of leadership to God the Father has upon it a psychological power that legitimizes masculine leadership in the home (social authority) and masculine leadership of the nation (political authority). She continues: "The affirmation of female power contained in the Goddess symbol has both psychological and political consequences."[9]

America saw these "political consequences" manifested when the feminist movement manipulated Anita Hill into testifying against Supreme Court Justice Clarence Thomas during his confirmation hearing. That hearing represented a meltdown of the political process of the United States.

The political process was turned into a nightly news showdown of Hill vs. Thomas in an attempt to assassinate the character of a good and godly man and an honorable jurist. Liberal interest groups and their hired guns spent three months digging in the dirt like maggots working a bloated corpse, asking "Have you got anything we can use to stop Thomas?

"Then, seemingly out of nowhere, came Anita Hill with wild stories about pornography and sexual harassment, stories that mutated and changed at least five times during that week in October, becoming ever more sordid. Though she had earlier refused to say such things to a female FBI investigator behind closed doors, and had never revealed them even to close friends, she said them before a packed hearing room and to millions of television viewers."[10]

Where *did* Anita HIll come from? "Leftist interest groups first unearthed Anita Hill and were actively involved in preparing the ambush. Nan Aron of the Alliance for Justice was the casting director, 'discovering' Anita Hill as early as July, and alerting Senator Metzenbaum's staff."[11]

Also "working on" Hill's testimony were the president of the radical feminist Women's Legal Defense Fund and the director of the National Abortion Rights Action League. A six-month investigation points out that, willingly or not, Anita Hill was part of a set-up.

Who set up the political ambush of Clarence Thomas? The feminists. Why? To control the Supreme Court and prevent *Roe v. Wade* from being overturned. To guarantee the murder of 1.5 million babies in America every year. Through what power? The power of witchcraft manifested in manipulation, intimidation and domination.

That was the driving spirit behind the character assassination of Clarence Thomas. You have to see the living devil in that. Every day that *Roe v. Wade* stays in place is another day Satan has to murder the future hope of America, our children.

What is the next goal of the feminist movement? To put enough women in Congress to guarantee the success of the feminist agenda. This election year there are 150 feminists running for Congress and 20 running for the Senate. Do not sell them short. They're well organized, highly funded, and there are a lot more of them than you think.

## The beginning of the battle of the sexes

Where did the battle of the sexes begin? Let's look at Genesis, the book of beginnings, because that's where it all started.

> *And God said, Let us make man in our image, after our likeness: and let them have dominion...So God cre-ated man in his own image, in the image of God created he him: male and female created he them.*
> Genesis 1:26-27

It was God's plan for man and woman to be co-regents over his creation. In Genesis 2:18 God said, "It is not good that the man should be alone; I will make him a help meet for him." Some people have said God knew man would need help to meet the car note, help to meet the boat note, and help to meet the house note. That's not what God is talking about.

A "help meet" for him, simply means a" helper suitable" for him. God created a co-regent for man, someone to be a help not a hindrance, a companion not a competitor.

Then in Genesis 3, the serpent seduced Eve into sin. How did he do it? He attacked the word of God. The first thing that came out of his mouth was, "Hath God said?" Six thousand years later, Satan is still attacking the word of God.

That's why humanists hate the Bible. They oppose the word of God, because it has the ability to say what is right and wrong. It has the ability to set moral absolutes, and humanists do not want any authority greater than their own. They don't want God Almighty to tell them they're wrong, or for the church to say they're wrong, or for Congress to say they're wrong. They just want to do what's right in their own eyes and be self-justified. (There's a good description of them in Romans 1:22-25.)

I've got news for the humanists. God's word has outlasted the Greeks and the Romans, it has endured the Nazis, and it will endure the humanists and the feminists. It has already buried the Communists, and when America no longer exists, the word of God will still be the law of God. When you attack the word of God, you're up against something that's stronger than you are and will outlast you.

How did the curse of sin happen? The woman, Eve, began to take the spiritual lead in the decision-making. She made some big decisions without taking her husband into consideration. These decisions led to rebellion against God's commands.

All Eve would have had to say was, "I don't talk to snakes without consulting my husband." Everything would have been great. Ladies, if you will follow the same policy, it will save you a lot of trouble. When you're faced with a major decision, consult your husband first.

Whenever a snake knocks on your door and says, "Ma'am, we've surveyed the neighborhood, and your neighbors say you are wonderful, charming, intelligent, gracious and a leader of leaders. Therefore, for $110 a month we would like to leave these free magazines with you," don't say, "Bring them in, you've described me perfectly." Tell that snake, "I'll talk to my husband about it."

The curse happened when the woman took the lead. Adam's sin was not that he submitted to Eve's need but to Eve's lead. Do you see the difference between that?

When you look at the Bible record of trouble, it started when the husband submitted to the wife's lead. (Men, you need to remember that your wife can't follow a parked car. So don't expect her to follow unless you're willing to lead.)

Adam submitted to Eve and the punishment is that every crumb of bread that goes into your mouth is earned by the sweat of your brow. It was God's intention that you and I sit in the vineyard and eat grapes and pet the lions and have a wonderful life. But this klutz Adam went over and ate the apple, and because of that we work eighty hours a week. And when I get to heaven, my personal assignment is going to be to kick old Adam right in the shins.

The second husband that followed the lead of his wife was Abraham. God promised Abraham and Sarah a child. But they were past their child-bearing years. Sarah said, "Look, apparently I'm not going to have a baby, so it appears to me that if you are going to have an heir, you should have a child with my servant Hagar."

Abraham said, "Sounds like the will of God to me." So Hagar has a baby and when Ishmael is about twelve years old Sarah decides she has had enough of this snippety servant and her son, so she says, "Throw them out." And Abraham again submitted to her leadership and did just that. (The story is in Genesis 16.)

Do you know who Ishmael is? He is the father of the Arab nations. Isaac, the son later born to Abraham and Sarah, is the father of the Jewish nations. The Jews and the Arabs are still going at each other and the whole Middle East crisis started right here in the book of Genesis because a husband followed the lead of his wife and not God.

Don't ever say, "Well, this is just a little family dispute and it doesn't affect anybody but us." Here's one family feud that affected the entire planet Earth.

Isaac was deceived by Rebekah concerning Jacob and the birthright. The result was that Jacob went into exile and Isaac never saw him again. Rebekah died under a divine curse and Esau and his descendants became slaves forever.

King Ahab listened to Jezebel and brought Ashtoreth and Baal worship into Israel. Jezebel killed the prophets. She controlled the church. She manipulated the government through her husband and promoted the goddess cult.

When you read the Old Testament, it is a sad story of one man after another who capitulated spiritual responsibility to his wife. We're still doing the same thing today in this nation.

For example, the Bible says, "*Fathers*, provoke not your children to wrath: but bring them up in the nurture and admonition of the Lord" (Eph. 6:4). Yet we have assigned the spiritual growth of our children to the mothers. "Honey, you take them to church. I'm going fishing."

Let me tell you something, fathers: God places the spiritual well-being of your children squarely on your shoulders, not your wife's. God expects you to get off the golf course and *you* take the children to God's house. You teach them the word of God.

## God's chain of authority

God established a chain of authority in his word. Look at 1 Corinthians 11:3, "The head of every man is Christ; and the head of the woman is the man; and the head of Christ is God." Here's the order: God the Father (and how that title irritates the feminist mentality), Jesus Christ the Son, then husband, then wife.

Paul reinforces God's order of authority in other writings:

> *Wives, submit yourselves unto your own husbands, as unto the Lord. For the husband is the head of the wife,*

*even as Christ is the head of the church.* Ephesians 5:22-23

Peter reinforces the divine order:

> *Likewise, ye wives, be in subjection to your own husbands; that, if any obey not the word, they also may without the word be won by the conversation of the wives; While they behold your chaste conversation coupled with fear. Whose adorning let it not be that outward adorning of plaiting the hair, and of wearing of gold, or of putting on of apparel; But let it be the hidden man of the heart, in that which is not corruptible, even the ornament of a meek and quiet spirit, which is in the sight of God of great price.* 1 Peter 3:1-4

It says that a believing woman can lead an ungodly husband to the Lord by her loving conduct. That's what "conversation" means; it refers to behavior not speech. An ungodly man can be won to the Lord through the "meek and quiet spirit" of a godly woman.

A "meek and quiet spirit." Does that describe the feminist movement? Hardly. But it describes the spirit of the woman in whom Jesus is Lord.

In Paul's pastoral instructions to Timothy, he gives a very clear position on God's directions for widows and younger women.

> *Let not a widow be taken into the number under threescore years old, having been the wife of one man, Well reported of for good works; if she have brought up children, if she have lodged strangers, if she have washed the saints' feet, if she have relieved the afflicted, if she have diligently followed every good work. But the younger widows refuse: for when they have begun to wax wanton against Christ, they will marry.* 1 Timothy 5:9-11

The older widows, those over 60 (threescore), were to be provided for by the church, if they had no family to take care of them. But, Paul said, it is under God's economy that younger women should remarry when their husbands died.

Compare this passage with Titus 2:3-5 where it says the older women are to teach the younger women to be sober, to love their husbands and children and to be keepers of the home.

In a society that's supposed to be so brilliant, why do we teach young women to be bankers, engineers, doctors and lawyers (and there's nothing wrong with that), but there is no one in or out of the church to teach them to love their husbands and children and to be keepers of the home?

When they get married they have absolutely no basis for knowing what God wants them to do. They go into a marriage knowing only what they've learned in a secular university saturated with humanism, where they won't learn the first thing about keeping a marriage together. It is no wonder the American home is falling apart.

## The curse of female domination

The curse for Eve's part in the rebellion against God is found in Genesis 3:6—

> Unto the woman he said, I will greatly multiply thy sorrow and thy conception; in sorrow thou shalt bring forth children; and thy desire shall be to thy husband, and he shall rule over thee.

The word "desire" here has nothing to do with sexual desire. Sexual desire is not a curse, it is God's plan. The word in Hebrew is *teshûqâh*, which means to rule or dominate. The curse is that the woman would seek to dominate the man, but that the man would rule over her.

Why did Paul say, "I suffer not a woman to...usurp authority over the man" (1 Tim. 2:12)? He knew it was the carnal instinct of women to try to do that very thing.

A fallen woman seeks to dominate. But the man has a God-given assignment to rule the house. Can you see the conflict there? It's immediate and instantaneous. The feminist movement today is throwing off authority in rebellion against God's pattern for the family.

God's plan is for the wife to submit to a loving husband. But when the husband tries to rule without love, you have the ingredients for a perpetual dog fight.

Some ladies say, "Well, I can't submit." If you are spirit filled it is not a problem. But if you are controlled by the spirit of rebellion and the spirit of witchcraft and the spirit of carnality, then you're right. Get ready for a fight. Call your lawyer and get your boxing gloves on, because it's not going to get any better.

Satan's plan for the wife from Genesis to this moment is to be in conflict with masculine leadership. Read it all through the book of Genesis. Genesis 3 is "man vs. woman." Genesis 4 is "polygamy." Now there's conflict in the home. Genesis 9 is "pornography." Genesis 16 is "adultery." Genesis 19 is "homosexuality." Genesis 34 is "fornication." Genesis 38 is "incest and prostitution." Genesis 39 is "seduction."

Why this continual conflict against marriage? Because if Satan can destroy the family, he can destroy the church. And if he can destroy the church, he can destroy the purpose of God. That's why.

In the 1990s we live in a demonic society saturated with pornography, adultery, fornication, homosexuality, incest, prostitution, drugs, alcohol, divorce—all these things destroy the fabric of the home. They are viruses that will kill a marriage. Books, movies and television mock what is pure and holy in a marriage and exalt the spirit of rebellion against the will of God.

You watch some television program written by some secular humanist and you hear some smart, cutting line from a wife about her husband, or from a husband about his wife, and you think, "That's what I need to say next time old so-and-so gets out of line." You store that in your memory bank and rehearse the line.

See how far off you are from mutual submission through love? Too often the marriage becomes a war zone and the devil is feeding your mind with bitter, vicious things to say to your partner. Words have power. They can rip and devour a relationship. Satan's strategy is to get you to tear each other down and rip each other apart—that brings glory to him.

God is fighting back with Ephesians 5, his plan of mutual submission for the husband and wife.

## God's plan for the husband and wife

Nearly every week that goes by I get a phone call or a letter that says, "I saw on this talk show where I ought to be thus and so." Quit getting your spiritual leadership from television sitcoms or talk shows. Phil Donahue does not know how to keep your marriage together. St. Paul does.

*...Submitting yourselves one to another in the fear of God. Wives, submit yourselves unto your own husbands, as unto the Lord. For the husband is the head of the wife, even as Christ is the head of the church: and he is the saviour of the body. Therefore as the church is subject unto Christ, so let the wives be to their own husbands in every thing.*

*Husbands, love your wives, even as Christ also loved the church, and gave himself for it; That he might sanctify and cleanse it with the washing of water by the word, That he might present it to himself a glorious church, not having spot, or wrinkle, or any such thing; but that it should be holy and without blemish. So ought men to love their wives as their own bodies.*

*He that loveth his wife loveth himself. For no man ever yet hated his own flesh; but nourisheth and cherisheth it, even as the Lord the church: For we are members of his body, of his flesh, and of his bones.*

*For this cause shall a man leave his father and mother, and shall be joined unto his wife, and they two shall be one flesh. This is a great mystery: but I speak concerning Christ and the church. Nevertheless let every one of you in particular so love his wife even as himself; and the wife see that she reverence her husband.* Ephesians 5:21-33

God's plan is for the wife to submit to her husband. Wife, quit taking direction from another man about anything. Husband, if you have a problem that involves a woman, go to her husband, not to her. If you get involved in a situation that involves another man's wife, go to her husband and solve the problem through him and not around him.

And if you have a controversy with someone, do not send your wife to resolve it, wimp. Some husbands are too chicken to stand up and face the music, so they send their wives out in front of them to go take the heat. Then they'll come around and say something so nicely like, "I just don't know how this controversy ever got started." It got started because you're such a chicken.

*Wives, submit yourselves unto your own husbands, as it is fit in the Lord. Husbands, love your wives, and be not bitter against them. Children, obey your parents in all things: for this is well-pleasing unto the Lord.* Colossians 3:18-20

Here is God's plan for the family in a nutshell. Verse 18 says that it is "fitting" for wives to submit to their husbands. It is fitting in all ages, even in the 1990s, because it is God's plan. It works.

*In like manner also, that women adorn themselves in modest apparel, with shamefacedness and sobriety; not with braided hair, or gold, or pearls, or costly array; But (which becometh women professing god- liness) with good works. Let the woman learn in silence with all subjection. But I suffer not a woman to teach, nor to usurp authority over the man, but to be in silence.* 1 Timothy 2:9-12

To dress in modest apparel is to treat your womanhood with love and respect. Your manner of dress says something about you. I have a psychology text that says bizarre dress is a sign of being mentally disturbed. If that's true, half of the world is crazy.

Wife, your dress is to be modest. It is not to be advertising. When you walk down the street in clothes the sum of which would not make a man's necktie, you are advertising. When you drag your moving billboard in front of a man with normal hormones, sparks are going to fly. "Well, I never expected him to look at me." Oh yes, you did. I was born recently, but not last night. He's looking and you like it.

Your outward adornment is not to be gaudy or costly, but becoming to good works. In Bible times (before there were banks that were failing), women made gold rings and wove them in their hair. It was a pentecostal-type bun of gold that was virtually theft-proof. If a thief tried to pull the jewels out of her hair, the wife would scream and that husband would be all over him like a duck on a June bug.

It also was a manifestation of what you were worth. A woman who wore gold in her hair gave her husband's Dun & Bradstreet rating when she walked into church. That hasn't stopped. It's still going on today.

## Women in culture then and now

What does 1 Timothy 2:11 mean when it says that women are to learn in silence and subjection? In orthodox synagogues, men sat on one side and women on the other. In Paul's time, if a woman did not understand what the rabbi was teaching, she would look across the aisle and ask her husband, "What did he say?"

Paul was saying that when you go to church, be quiet. Wait until you get home to ask your husband questions, because you can't get it settled in church.

Verse 12 has been misappropriated to say that women can not teach anything at all in the church. That is plain wrong and ignores the examples of Priscilla and Phoebe and a number of other women described in the epistles as Paul's "co-workers."

There is a ministry gift of teaching that is legitimate for both men and women. My own mother is a gifted teacher of God's word. She was a Bible school instructor before I was born, and she shared the teaching responsibilities in my father's pastoral ministry. What Paul is saying here is that a woman may not exercise spiritual authority or pastor a church.

Did women in the first century live in a culture that made submitting to their husbands a lot easier? No way.

History supports the fact that women of that day refused to have babies because it ruined their figures. Sound familiar? Women of that day competed in feats of strength in an attempt to show equality with the male. They wrestled with each other, fought with swords and helmets, went pig hunting with spears wearing only loin cloths, then ate the pig and got drunk. Why? Because that's what men did.

Housewives in Athens sold themselves into prostitution with slaves. Lesbianism was rampant. Divorce and drunkenness were epidemic. The female motto in the Athenian culture was, "Live your own life."

Does it strike you as funny that that's exactly the same thing we see here today? Women's liberation is not new. It started in Genesis 3:6, it was alive in New Testament times, and it lives in our day.

Wives are given a choice between rebellion against God's plan or submission to God's plan. If you rebel against God, then you have given your marriage over to the spirit of witchcraft. If you submit to God's plan you will have peace, love and joy of the Holy Spirit.

Satan comes to every woman just as he came to Eve. "Would you like to live your own life? Would you like to be like God?" He will appeal to your ego and do everything he can to seduce you away from your husband's authority.

God calls women to be submitted to a loving husband, to be spirit filled, to be a godly helpmate, to be pure and chaste, to be loving and gracious to children and parents, to care for widows and orphans and to show hospitality to all.

There is a radical feminist movement with a plan to tear the nation up and control it. The church of Jesus Christ must commit itself to absolute obedience to the word of God, because if you can be manipulated and intimidated by threats or lies, you will be.

If your commitment to Christ is so feeble that you look for a way to escape controversy any time there's a conflict between the kingdom of God and the kingdom of darkness, you won't make it to heaven. From now until the rapture of the church it's going to be a spiritual street fight. So put on the whole armor of God. Gussy up and get ready!

## Notes

1. Christ, Carol P. & Plaskow, Judith, editors. *Womanspirit Rising: A Feminist Reader In Religion.* (New York: HarperCollins Publishers, 1992), p. 262.

2. Ardinger, Barbara, PhD. *A Woman's Book of Rituals and Celebrations.* (San Rafael: New World Library, 1992), p. 36.

3. *Womanspirit Rising*, p. 274.

4. *Womanspirit Rising*, p. 54-55.

5. *Womanspirit Rising*, p. 259-268.

6. *Womanspirit Rising*, p. 120-121.

7. *Womanspirit Rising*, p. 123.

8. *Womanspirit Rising*, p. 275, emphasis in original.

9. *Womanspirit Rising*, p. 278.

10. "Anita Hill: Feminist Fraud" by Thomas L. Jipping. *Christian American*, July-August 1992, page 5.

11. *ibid.*

# Chapter 4

# *The Environmentalist Agenda*

**D**uring the recent Earth Summit environmental conference in Rio de Janeiro, I opened the San Antonio *Express-News* and saw a picture of the participants. They were kneeling in a circle drawn on the ground, and the question immediately came to mind, To whom were they praying?

I recognized the significance of the magic circle used in satanic and occultic worship. A circle is drawn on the ground and the participants pray for power to be released in the circle. To see the environmentalists at the Earth Summit involved in what appeared to be ritualistic worship caused me to investigate the Earth Summit and the environmental movement. What I discovered is shocking, and something every American needs to know.

Let me start out by saying this about conservation: I'm for clean water, clean air and the preservation of our natural resources. Let's recycle what needs to be recycled to save what needs to be saved. But the environmental movement is not about conservation. It's about creating an environmental juggernaut that marries the New World Order crowd and the New Age occultists with the objective of bringing about a global crisis that can only be solved by a one-world government.

## Objectives of the environmental movement

The objectives of the environmental movement are to control the U. S. economy through governmental regulations and to control the birth rate in the U. S. through abortion and restrictive population control methods. There are many in the United States who would like to see China's restrictive policies adopted across the globe. How do they control population in China? The official government policy is "one couple, one child," and it is enforced through mandatory abortion and sterilization. Female infanticide is common in China, since a couple is only permitted to have one child and boys are more highly valued than girls.

Another objective of the environmental movement is to re-distribute the wealth of America to third world nations through the control of the United Nations without interference from the United States. Maurice Strong, Secretary General of UNCED (United Nations Conference on Environmental Development) and mastermind of the Earth Summit in Rio said, "The Earth Summit must establish a whole new basis for relations between rich and poor, North and South, including a concerted attack on poverty as a central priority for the 21st century."[1] He also promised that Planned Parenthood would be an important item on the agenda.

Do you remember Lyndon B. Johnson and his War on Poverty? After throwing hundreds of billions of dollars into poverty programs there are more poor people in America today than when LBJ started his War on Poverty. I also want you to know that America's poor people are rich when measured against the poor of the world.

The fact is that poverty will never be eliminated. The Bible says there will always be poor people (Deut. 15:11, Matt. 26:11). Why is this true? Because character cannot be purchased with a federal grant from Washington, D.C. The people who broke into the stores in Los Angeles and stole everything in sight were not irate citizens. They were thieves looking for a reason to manifest their character.

You cannot eliminate poverty, because you cannot motivate lazy people to work by giving them money taken from those who are willing to work. That's against the word of God. The Bible says that if you don't work, you shouldn't eat (2 Thess. 3:10).

You cannot eliminate poverty, because drug addiction brings poverty and drug addiction is a choice. It is a choice manifested by poor character. You cannot eliminate poverty because alcoholism is a choice. And you cannot remove alcoholism with a federal grant.

You cannot eliminate poverty, because gambling brings poverty. Americans are addicted to the hope of getting something for nothing. That's not God's system. God's system is to earn it "by the sweat of your brow" (Gen. 3:19). God's plan for wealth does not include a lottery system.

You cannot eliminate poverty, because crime brings poverty. Idolatry brings poverty. God brings poverty to those who forsake him, and America is fast becoming a nation of idolators. "Blessed is the nation whose God is the Lord" (Psa. 33:12). That no longer describes America. The problem in America is that times are desperate but the church of Jesus Christ is not. The America that I know and love is dying, and the church slumbers while it happens.

## The Earth Summit: "Save Mother Earth"

The objective of the Earth Summit sponsored by UNCED was to set the stage for the "Save Mother Earth" crisis, which is more media hype than environmental fact. The Earth Summit was a marriage of the occult and New Age with the environmental movement.

Why hold this international meeting in Rio de Janeiro? The name of this city means "River of January." The month of January was named after the ancient Roman god Janus, who was the keeper of the gate to the next life. Thus, the River of Janus (or

Rio de Janeiro) is the gate through which one enters the world of the gods in the New Age.

Those who went to Rio opened themselves, willingly or unwillingly, to the invasion of demon spirits, because the New Age is a doctrine of demons. The apostle Paul said, "In the latter times some shall depart from the faith, giving heed to seducing spirits and doctrines of demons" (1 Tim. 4:1). A doctrine of demons is a teaching that you can gain access to God by a means other than Jesus Christ. That's what the New Age teaches. If you are participating in the New Age movement, you are participating in a doctrine of demons, whether you know it or not. You are damning your immortal soul and committing spiritual adultery.

## Manipulation through a created crisis

How do the environmentalists hope to manipulate America and redistribute the world's wealth to "Save Mother Earth"? You manipulate the masses by creating a crisis for which you have the solution before the crisis begins. Adolf Hitler was a master of this technique. He conquered most of Europe with threats, simply because world leaders shook like Jello in front of him. He created crises for which he had solutions all the time. The environmental movement is a classic example of creating a crisis for which you already have a solution—the solution always being more government control and eventually a global, one-world government.

A secret study was commissioned by the federal government under President Kennedy. This special study group met for the first time in 1963 at Iron Mountain, New York. Their purpose was to structure the future of the world. A top-secret document was later issued by the group, titled "Report From Iron Mountain on the Possibility and Desirability of Peace." This report looked forward to the time when global disarmament would no longer serve as the crisis of choice for the New World Order crowd. (And with the collapse of the Soviet Union and the fall of communism, global disarmament no longer seems as critical as it once was.)

The Iron Mountain report states,

> *It may be, for instance, that gross pollution of the environment can eventually replace the possibility of mass destruction by nuclear weapons as the principal apparent threat to the survival of the species. Poisoning of the air, and of the principal sources of the food and water supply ... at first glance would seem promising in this respect; it constitutes a threat that can be dealt with only through social organization and political power ... But it will be a generation to a generation and a half before environmental pollution, however severe, will be sufficiently menacing on a global scale, to offer a possible basis for solutions.*[2]

Note the wording of this secret report: "the principal *apparent* threat." In other words, we want to manipulate people with the fear that we're going to poison the earth with pollution. Then we'll use that fear to control their lives, control their income, control the economy, and with that control we can do what we want to do. The environmental crisis is a *created* crisis, and it was planned nearly thirty years ago.

> *The* Report *also called for mandatory population control to replace the 'genetically regressive' effects of the war system: 'There is no question but that a universal requirement that procreation be limited to the products of artificial insemination would provide a fully adequate substitute control for population levels. Such a reproductive system would, of course, have the added advantage of being susceptible to direct eugenic management. The ecological function of war under these circumstances would not only be superseded but surpassed in effectiveness.*[3]

Again, note the wording: *eugenic management*. This is what Hitler engaged in, eugenic management.

Following the Iron Mountain report, members of the CFR (Council on Foreign Relations) and the Trilateral commission began writing that we would have to do away with national sovereignty to pave the way for a global government. Richard Gardner, former US Ambassador to Italy said in 1974, "We must make an end run around national sovereignty, eroding it piece by piece."[4]

What does it mean to erode national sovereignty? That means America's ability to control her destiny must be removed from the people—that's you. It means that the Constitution of the United States must become inferior to the United Nations charter. Think back just a few months to the Persian Gulf crisis and remember how the media machine fell in line with the New World Order crowd, exalting and eulogizing the United Nations. Let me tell you, dear hearts, the United Nations has been the United Nothing for the last thirty years. Do we really want these people running the world? No way.

Eroding the national sovereignty means making the Bill of Rights null and void—that which has been paid for in the blood, sweat and tears of America's servicemen across the world wiped out of history with the sweep of one pen. Get your ears open. When you hear a politician talking about making "an end run around national sovereignty," realize that man is not for you. He is trying to destroy America and you need to vote him out of office, or vote the politicians who put him there out of office.

Lawrence Rockefeller, another rich and powerful globalist, said in 1976, "Either through voluntary discipline or state compulsion," human society will have to be reconstructed. He also said that it would be necessary to use "authoritarian control" to "save the earth."[5] State compulsion means force. Now doesn't that make you feel safe to know that world leaders want to use force to reconstruct our society into their one-world vision!

The environmental crisis is phony; it was created to manipulate you. Donald McAlvany says,

> *The environmental crisis is a giant scam, a sham, a staged pseudo-crisis (like the pseudo-coup in the Soviet Union in August '91) designed to give national and international government bureaucrats and*

*globalists the excuse to impose socialistic, communist
bloc-type controls on people, business, private property and virtually all aspects of our lives—"in order to
save Planet Earth for future generations."[6]*

## What is the truth about global warming?

Is there any truth to the environmental crisis? Is Planet Earth
in danger? Global warming and the so-called "greenhouse effect"
are being de-bunked by leading scientists, along with the hole-
in-the-ozone crisis and the endangered species crisis. Robert
Jastrow, a distinguished physicist and astronomer recently said,

*Global warming may be due to changes in the sun
rather than the 'greenhouse gases' that most scientists
say have caused it. ... All the evidence suggests that
"greenhouse" warming is considerably smaller than
... predicted up to this time.[7]*

Jastrow went on to say that plants on earth are actually starving
for carbon dioxide. "But if you say that, it so counters the general
impression that you lose credibility."[8] Who put that general
impression out there? The media machine. They have so promoted
the idea of global warming from burning fossil fuels that repu-
table scientists cannot dispute it without losing credibility. A
large number of eminent scientists do not agree with the un-
supported assumptions of global warming. But you won't hear
them interviewed on ABC, CBS, NBC or CNN, and you won't
read their opinions in you local newspaper, unless the story is
stuck back on page 43 or hidden somewhere. Science is supposed
to be about exploring all the possibilities on an equal playing
field. But not any more.

## The major players in the environmental movement

The identification of the following four groups in the environ-mental movement is taken from the *McAlvany Intelligence Advisor*, quoted previously, and a book by Berit Kjos, *Under the Spell of Mother Earth*. The major players in the environmental movement can be broken down as follows:

(1) *The Conservation movement*, including such groups as the Audobon Society and the Sierra Club. These were originally the most sane people in the movement. However, they are in danger of being taken over by the more radical environmentalists.

(2) *The "Radical Green" sector*, which carries out acts of vandalism to protect endangered species like spotted owls. These people think nothing of killing human children in the womb, a truly "endangered species," but will save the lives of the spotted owl at all costs. "Their agenda goes far beyond ecology, to gay rights and the abolition of nations and private property."[9]

(3) *The "deep ecology" sector*, which links the movement to the New Age and the occult. Many of these environmentalists are involved in pagan religions. (Remember the self-proclaimed pagans in Chapter 3 who described witchcraft as "an ancient, earth-based religion"?) Most environmentalists in this sector worship Gaia, the feminine spirit of the earth. The name of their goddess, Gaia, comes from the Greek word for earth. She is also sometimes referred to as the Mother Goddess, Mother Earth or Mother Nature. So when you read a newspaper report that mentions Mother Nature, or Gaia, or the feminine spirit of the earth, interpret that to mean a demon spirit.

(4) *The eastern establishment* and liberals in America and Europe. These are the people I call the New World Order crowd. They include the members of the Council on Foreign Relations, the Trilateral Commission, the Club of Rome and prominent globalists already mentioned.

All these diverse groups have a common objective. They hate private property owners. They hate the free enterprise system. They portray all businessmen as evil, greedy villains. And they want to stop all industrial growth (i.e. your job) through restrictive environmental laws. Why? So they can control the economy, the government, and you.

What kind of financial power does the environmental movement have? Environmentalists control four times the amount of money of the Republican and Democratic parties combined. Congressman William Dannemeyer of California says they have so much financial clout that he calls it a political party: the Environmental Party.

## A revival of pantheism

The spiritual force behind the environmental movement is a revival of pantheism, a key component of New Age religion. Pantheism is the belief that God is not personal, but an impersonal force present everywhere and in everything in the universe. That's why pantheists worship the earth, because they believe god is present in the rocks, dirt, grass and trees. So don't hurt the trees—that's god! Pantheism is another doctrine of demons, teaching access to God by a means other than Jesus Christ.

Hollywood is saturated with occultists and environmentalists. Did you ever wonder why movies about American Indians, such as *Dances with Wolves*, are so popular now? Indians are spiritualists and pantheists. They worship "The Great Spirit," the god who is present everywhere in everything. That's the mentality Hollywood wants to project to America. All these movie makers and rock stars who are "saving the rain forests" and "preserving indigenous cultures" are really promoting pantheism and nature worship. Just like it says in Romans 1:25, they have "changed the truth of God into a lie and worshiped and served the creature [or creation] more than the Creator."

There is one God. He is God the Father, and he sits in the heavens—he is not disguised as a tree or a rock. He is the Lord of Hosts and beside him there is no other god. Romans 8:22-23 says that all of creation is groaning and waiting for the day of his return. He will return as the King of King and Lord of Lords. He will set up a New World Order in the New Jerusalem and I'm going to be a part of it.

## The future of planet earth

The Earth Summit in Rio de Janeiro was not about clean air, clean water, acid rain or global warming. It was about how to control the wealth of America and redistribute it to third world countries at the expense of the American taxpayer. It was about world leaders creating a massive international media platform to attack America for her alleged crimes against the global environment. It was a marriage of the New Agers and the New World Order crowd.

Contrary to what was reported from Rio, America has the cleanest environment of any industrial nation on the face of the earth. All you will hear about in the media is the manufactured environmental crisis, but it's a lie.

What is the future of the planet? Here it is in a nutshell: "The earth is the Lord's, and the fullness thereof; the world, and they that dwell therein" (Psa. 24:1).

Do you understand that? *The earth is the Lord's.* He does not need the New World Order crowd. He does not need the New Age. He does not need Gaia-worshipping pagans to help him maintain his creation. He is not in heaven drinking Maalox over the ozone problem or global warming. The only time global warming has ever occurred is when God the Father rained fire and brimstone on Sodom and Gomorrah exactly like he said he would.

*The earth is the Lord's.* He is in charge. Aren't you glad some nitwit bureaucrat in Washington does not have the responsibility for going out every morning and adjusting the ocean tides? God is in charge of nature. He divided the Red Sea for Moses—that's being in control of nature. He destroyed the world by a flood, just like he said he would. Read it in Genesis 7 and 8. It says that in a certain month, on a certain day, at a certain hour, the fountains of the deep were opened up because God controlled the flood-waters.

God did not sit there in heaven and hit the wrong button and say, "Oops. I'm sorry." He destroyed the world by a flood because he said he would. It happened just like he wanted it to happen because he's in charge of the earth. He held the sun still for Joshua. That's control.

Jesus Christ stood on the bow of a boat in the Sea of Galilee and said, "Peace, be still!" and the wind and the waves obeyed him. Gaia didn't do it. Witchcraft didn't do it. The Son of God did it. He is not nature, he is above nature. He is the foundation of the church, and the church will not collapse. The church of Jesus Christ will not be intimidated or brainwashed by the environmentalists or the major media.

Listen to God's weather report. "The Lord hath his way in the whirlwind and in the storm" (Nahum 1:3). That means he controls the whirlwind; he's in charge of the storm. "He maketh the storm a calm, so that the waves thereof are still" (Psalms 107:29). "Behold, the Lord rideth upon a swift cloud" (Isaiah 19:1). When tornadoes sweep across America and the winds shake the earth, God is not worried. He's in control.

God will use nature to announce the Second Coming. The signs of Jesus Christ's return to earth will be signs of nature. Why do you suppose that is? I believe God knew from the beginning that some pagan cretins were going to come along with a doctrine about nature worship and the spirit of the earth. And God will prove to anyone with the intellectual capacity of a stump that he is in absolute control.

Acts 2:19-20 says, "And I will show wonders in heaven above, and signs in the earth beneath ... the sun shall be turned into darkness, and the moon into blood, before that great and notable day of the Lord." God says, "Just before I return, I'm going to put on a fireworks display in the heavenlies that will outdo Disneyland. So pay attention, all you tree-hugging Gaia worshippers."

## The end of the environmental issue

The earth is the Lord's. He is in control. At the end of time, at his appointed time, the earth's atmosphere will be irreparably polluted by nuclear war.

> *But the day of the Lord will come as a thief in the night; in the which the heavens shall pass away with a great noise, and the elements shall melt with fervent heat, the earth also and the works that are therein shall be burned up. ... Nevertheless we, according to his promise, look for new heavens and a new earth, wherein dwelleth righteousness.* 2 Peter 3:10, 13

The day of the Lord will come "as a thief in the night." That means suddenly, unexpectedly. The Bible also says, "For when they shall say, Peace and safety; then sudden destruction cometh upon them" (1 Thess. 5:3).

"The heavens shall pass away with a great noise," that's an explosion. "And the elements shall melt with fervent heat," which is exactly what happens in an atomic explosion. The bomb that fell on Hiroshima not only produced a "great noise," all the elements "melted with fervent heat" for one mile. Anything within one mile of that blast melted, whether it was steel or concrete. "The earth also and the works that are therein shall be burned up." Everything within 25 miles of Hiroshima caught on fire spontaneously, an exact picture of the heat described in 2 Peter 3:10.

The atomic warfare of the present makes what happened at Hiroshima seem like a firecracker by comparison. The earth's atmosphere will be destroyed in a nuclear explosion. That will be the end of the environmental issue. And there's not one thing you can do about it.

What happens after that? Look at Revelation 21:

> *And I saw a new heaven and a new earth: for the first heaven and the first earth were passed away; and there was no more sea ... And he that sat upon the*

*throne said, Behold, I make all things new.*
Rev. 21:1, 5

The Bible says that the first heaven and first earth were passed away. Gaia didn't make them pass away. Witchcraft didn't make them pass away. The New World Order and the radical environmentalists didn't make them pass away. God caused it to pass away.

"He that sat upon the throne said ... I make all things new." Gaia does not make all things new, nor does any sector of the environmental movement. The Living God, the Creator of heaven and earth, will make it as new as he did in the beginning of time.

## Notes

1. quoted in "Saving Mother Earth: The Environmental Juggernaut," *The McAlvany Intelligence Advisor,* July 1992, p. 9. (Donald S. McAlvany, Editor: P.O. Box 84904, Phoenix, AZ 85071)

2. ibid, p. 2. Also quoted in "The Report From Iron Mountain" by Randall J. Barnett, *Christian American,* July/August 1992, p. 28. (published by Christian Coalition, PO Box 1990, Chesapeake, VA 23327-1990)

3. Barnett, p. 28.

4. McAlvany, p. 2

5. ibid.

6. McAlvany, p. 3.

7. Associated Press, "Scientist links global warming to sun, not greenhouse gases." Express-*News*, San Antonio, Texas, August 1, 1992.

8. ibid.

9. McAlvany, p. 4.

## Chapter 5

# Capital
# Punishment

"**A**nd he that killeth any man shall surely be put to death" (Lev. 24:17). "Whoso sheddeth man's blood, by man shall his blood be shed" (Gen. 9:6). "He that smiteth a man, so that he die, shall be surely put to death" (Ex. 21:12).

You don't have to be a rocket scientist to read these verses and understand that the Bible supports the death penalty. But point this out to an opponent of capital punishment and you will hear in reply one of the few Bible verses that even secular humanists can quote: "Thou shalt not kill" (Ex. 20:13).

Does the Bible contradict itself? Does the sixth commandment mean that the Bible prohibits the death penalty in spite of the other verses that seem to support it? Not at all. The Bible does not contradict itself and a careful examination of scripture shows a consistent position against murder and for capital punishment when murder has been committed. There's the difference.

"Thou shalt not murder" would actually be a better translation of the sixth commandment. The Hebrew word translated *kill* in that verse is *rasah.* It has the specialized meaning of murder by an intentional, malicious act (as opposed to homicide or manslaughter).

Our legal concepts of murder and homicide were founded upon scriptural precepts. The Bible recognizes the difference between murder and homicide. It also specifies how murder is to be proved and how the death penalty is to be carried out in a capital crime.

When one person is killed by another person, it may or may not be a criminal offense. If the killer planned to kill his victim, it is premeditated murder, or murder with "malice aforethought." In other words, the intent of the killer determines the degree of the crime. If the killing was accidental, or was provoked by the victim, the crime is of a lesser degree.

The names of the offenses vary from state to state, but there are usually three or more classifications of homicide recognized: *capital murder* (that is murder for which the defendant may receive the death penalty), *murder one* and *murder two* (or several varying degrees of premeditated murder), and *voluntary* or *involuntary manslaughter* (an action or accident that caused an unintentional death).

## The Constitutional question

The Constitutional question of capital punishment has pretty much been settled. The moral issue, however, is still being debated. We will look at the Bible's position to settle the moral issue, but let's look briefly at the Constitutional question.

All of the recent Supreme Court cases have upheld the constitutionality of the death penalty. The Court has said, however, that the way the death penalty has been carried out in some states was unconstitutional.

Constitutional arguments against the death penalty are usually based on the eighth amendment, which forbids "cruel and unusual punishment." At the time the Constitution was written, capital punishment was not considered cruel, nor was it unusual.

Both the 5th and 14th amendments to the Constitution recognize the death penalty. These amendments say that a citizen cannot be deprived of life or liberty without "due process of law." In other words, before someone can be executed for a crime, certain legal requirements must be met.

The Supreme Court, however, has not always followed a "strict construction" method of interpreting the Constitution. Those who favor strict construction, usually conservatives, say the Constitution should be interpreted in light of what it meant to the Founding Fathers who wrote it. Those who are against a strict constructionist interpretation of the Constitution, usually liberals, say the Constitution must be viewed as a dynamic, changing document that reflects contemporary society.

*Count me on the side of the Founding Fathers.*

This same argument, by the way, takes place among interpreters of the Bible. Those who favor a literal or grammatical-historical interpretation of the Bible, usually conservative theologians, say we must examine the "plain meaning" of scripture and determine what the author intended to say to his readers. This does not mean the Bible has nothing to say to us today; it just means we need to interpret the Bible in the context of its original meaning to its original audience. Those who favor an allegorical method of interpretation, usually liberal theologians, say that there is a deeper spiritual or allegorical meaning beyond the literal meaning of scripture.

You won't have to think hard to figure out where I stand on this issue, either. *Count me on the side of those who believe the Bible literally means what it says.*


## Murder merits the death penalty

So what does the Bible say about capital punishment? The Bible says that the person who commits premeditated murder is to be put to death. Period.

We have already looked at some scriptures. "And he that killeth any man shall surely be put to death" (Lev. 24:17). "Whoso sheddeth man's blood, by man shall his blood be shed" (Gen. 9:6). Lengthier discussions of the death penalty are found in Exodus 21, Numbers 35 and Deuteronomy 19.

*He that smiteth a man, so that he die, shall be surely*

*put to death. And if a man lie not in wait, but God deliver him into his hand; then I will appoint thee a place whither he shall flee. But if a man come pre-sumptuously* [willfully] *upon his neighbor, to slay him with guile* [malice aforethought]*; thou shalt take him from mine altar, that he may die.*

*And he that smiteth his father, or his mother, shall be surely put to death. And he that stealeth* [kidnaps] *a man, and selleth him, or if he be found in his hand, he shall surely be put to death. And he that curseth his father, or his mother, shall surely be put to death.* Ex. 21:12-17

The primary principle of punishment in the Bible is propor-tionality. That means that the punishment must be proportionate to the crime committed. This is the "eye-for-an-eye" punishment the Bible teaches, found in the 21st chapter of Exodus:

*If men strive, and hurt a woman with child, so that her fruit depart from her, and yet no mischief follow: he shall be surely punished, according as the woman's husband will lay upon him; and he shall pay as the judges determine.*

*And if any mischief follow, then thou shalt give life for life. Eye for eye, tooth for tooth, hand for hand, foot for foot, burning for burning, wound for wound, stripe for stripe.* verses 22-25

This principle of proportionality has been recognized by our Supreme Court. That's why the range of crimes which merit the death penalty is actually quite narrow. The Court ruled, for instance, that imposing the death penalty for rape was a "grossly disproportionate" punishment. Capital punishment is usually limited to the murder or a law enforcement officer or to murder committed during a felony offense (such as armed robbery).

## The Bible prescribes death, not compensation

For bodily injury, compensation in money or kind could be given to the victim. But not for murder. Compensation in cases of murder would have made life cheap and allowed the rich to trample the rights of the poor. The Bible position on the death penalty actually gives equal status and protection to the poor.

Scripture says that premeditated murder justifies the death penalty because it is a punishment proportionate to the crime. Beyond that, the Bible's view of the utter sanctity of life required the murderer's death, because the shedding of innocent blood defiled the holiness of the land.

> *Thou shalt put away the guilt of innocent blood from Israel, that it may go well with thee.*  Deut. 19:13

> *So ye shall not pollute the land wherein ye are: for blood it defileth the land: and the land cannot be cleansed of the blood that is shed therein, but by the blood of him that shed it. Defile not therefore the land which ye shall inhabit, wherein I dwell: for I the Lord dwell among the children of Israel.*  Num. 35:32-34

A number of crimes warranted the death penalty in the Bible: murder, adultery, incest, sodomy, rape, kidnapping, witchcraft, blasphemy, and disobedience to parents. (Teenagers, think about that next time you decide to tell your parents off!)

## The avenger of blood

The death sentence for murder was carried out by the "avenger of blood" (Hebrew *go'el haddam*), who was the closest male relative of the victim. The *go'el* was the protector and defender of family interests; in this role he is sometimes referred to as the redeemer. He was responsible for protecting the property, liberty and posterity of his next of kin, in addition to his specialized role as avenger.

In the case of manslaughter, the avenger of blood could not retaliate against the killer, as long as the killer stayed within one of the designated cities of refuge. But if he left the city of refuge, the avenger of blood could execute him without fear of punishment. (See Numbers 35 and Deuteronomy 19.)

The image of the redeemer-avenger is several times used as a description of God's relationship to his people.

*Rejoice, O ye nations, with his people: for he will avenge the blood of his servants, and will render vengeance to his adversaries.* Deut. 32:43

*Wherefore should the heathen say, Where is their God? Let him be known among the heathen in our sight by the revenging of the blood of thy servants which is shed.* Psalm 79:10

*And I will feed them that oppress thee with their own flesh; and they shall be drunken with their own blood, as with sweet wine: and all flesh shall know that I the Lord am thy Savior and thy Redeemer, the mighty One of Jacob.* Isa. 49:26

*I saw under the altar the souls of them that were slain for the word of God, and for the testimony which they held: And they cried with a loud voice, saying, How long, O Lord, holy and true, dost thou not judge and avenge our blood on them that dwell on the earth?* Rev. 6:9-10

## Cities of refuge

Manslaughter is the term used to differentiate between an accidental homicide and a premeditated murder. The Bible established cities of refuge to protect the person who accidentally killed someone. The cold-blooded murderer, the one who killed with intent, was to be put to death. But the "manslayer," or one who accidentally caused a death, was to be protected from the avenger of blood.

> *Thou shalt prepare thee a way, and divide the coasts of thy land, which the Lord thy God giveth thee to inherit, into three parts, that every slayer may flee thither.*
>
> *And this is the case of the slayer, which shall flee thither, that he may live: Whoso killeth his neighbor ignorantly* [unawares], *whom he hated not in time past; As when a man goeth into the wood with his neighbor to hew wood, and his hand fetcheth a stroke with the axe to cut down the tree, and the head slippeth from the helve* [handle], *and lighteth upon his neighbor, that he die; he shall flee unto one of those cities, and live: Lest the avenger of blood pursue the slayer, while his heart is hot, and overtake him, because the way is long, and slay him; whereas he was not worthy of death, inasmuch as he hated him not in time past.*
>
> *Wherefore I command thee, saying, Thou shalt separate three cities for thee ... then shalt thou add three cities more for thee, beside these three: That innocent blood be not shed in thy land, which the Lord thy God giveth thee for an inheritance, and so blood be upon thee.*
>
> *But if any man hate his neighbor, and lie in wait for him, and rise up against him, and smite him mortally that he die, and fleeth into one of these cities: Then the elders of his city shall send and fetch him thence, and deliver him into the hand of the avenger of blood, that he may die. Thine eye shall not pity him, but thou shalt put away the guilt of innocent blood from Israel, that it may go well with thee.* Deut. 19:3-7, 9-13

God established these cities of refuge to protect those who did not deserve the death penalty. For example, if you and I are chopping wood together and the axe-head flies off and hits you in the head and kills you, I am not guilty of murder. It was an accident. I can flee to the nearest city of refuge and live safely there the rest of my life. Your avenger of blood cannot touch me. But if I venture outside the city of refuge, I am fair game for the avenger of blood.

Obviously there was no ACLU in Bible times. When you see capital punishment like God sees it, it becomes very clear. When you see it like the ACLU sees it, you might as well go to every penitentiary and turn loose every serial killer who's frustrated with society. I call the liberal view of capital punishment the "not enough cookies as a Boy Scout" theory. It is a total denial of responsibility for criminal conduct.

God, however, says punishment should be meted out according to responsibility. If I accidentally kill you, as in the axe-head example, I don't deserve the death penalty. But if I get in an argument with you over a baseball score and I pull a gun out and blow your head off, I have committed murder and have forfeited my right to live.

What about "jailhouse conversions," those who get saved while waiting on death row? They still deserve the death penalty. If they truly found Jesus, they will see him immediately upon execution. If they're running a scam and just trying to escape punishment by pretending to be converted, then they'll see the one they deserve to see. Don't bother sending cards and letters— I'm not going to change my mind.

*Bible Positions On Political Issues*

is also available on cassette tape.

Call or write for more information.

John Hagee Ministries

P.O. Box 1400

San Antonio, TX 78295

(210) 491-5100

# About the author...

Rev. John Hagee is a scholar, musician, athlete, evangelist, and above all, a pastor with a pastor's heart. A fourth-generation preacher in the tradition of his father and grandfathers before him, Hagee not only shepherds the 13,000-member, nondenominational Cornerstone Church in San Antonio, Texas, he is pastor to other pastors around the country through the Cornerstone Fellowship of Churches.

John Hagee Ministries produces three television programs that are seen throughout the Northern hemisphere. *Cornerstone* is a weekly broadcast of the Sunday morning service at Cornerstone Church. *John Hagee Today* is a teaching program aired Monday through Friday. *Cornerstone Live* is a live-via-satellite broadcast of the Sunday evening service from Cornerstone Church that can be seen by over five million homes with backyard satellite dishes.

Author of several books, John Hagee is a dynamic conference speaker whose straightforward style of preaching, laced with humor, brings refreshing biblical insight to contemporary problems. He is married to Diana Castro Hagee and they reside in San Antonio with their children Tish, Chris, Christina, Matthew and Sandy.